The Memory Pool

The Memory Pool
Reflections of Past~Forward

The Past~Forward Memoir Group

Edited by
Daiva Markelis

Copyright © 2014
All rights reserved

Cover design by Gaye Harrison

Cantraip Press, Ltd.
2317 Saratoga Place
Charleston, IL 61920

ISBN 978-0-9844281-5-1

LCCN 2014950530

To Lee Roll —
　　Wonderful writer,
　　　　Outstanding teacher,
　　　　　　Inspiration to us all.

Contents

Preface	1
Daiva Markelis	3
Acknowledgements	5
Above the Beach	7
Presbyterian Surprise	12
A Nostalgic Passion	15
The Menu	16
Phyllis Bayles	22
Singing to Fox and Other Adventures	25
A Very Dark Day in Charleston, Illinois, History	29
Bob Clapp	35
Wonderland Under	37
Testament	43
Lois Dickenson	48
A New World	49
Keeping Time	54
Mary Dwiggins	59
The Civil War and My Ancestors	61
My Mother	65
Hannah Eads	71
La Grange Park	73
Dad	78
Marty Gabriel	85
Harryetta	87
Leaving	93
Thanksgiving in 55 Words	94
Renaissance	95
Alone	102

Jane Cavins Gilbert	107
San Francisco Penny	109
Gaye Harrison	113
The Most Amazing Lady I Have Ever Known	115
Dorothy Helland	119
The Salesman	121
A School Day	126
Paddling to Canada	127
Bill Heyduck	131
Forgotten Memory	133
Windows	136
Madeline Ignazito	138
More Blessed to Give Than to Receive	141
Love and Marriage	147
Helen Krehbiel-Reed	148
Happy Trails	149
Photographs	154
Amy Lynch	158
A Hair-Raising Experience	159
Old Blue Eyes	165
Janet Messenger	169
Bob and Tom	171
Bus Stop	173
Please Help	174
My Special Shoes	175
Sometimes at Night	178
Johnni Olds	179
Afghan	181
Peggy Perkins	183
Eddie Thompson	185
David R. Pollard	188
How I Learned to Play Guitar Off the TV	189

Turquoise and Race Horses	193
Julie Rea	197
The Love of My Life	199
Sophie	200
Denise Shumaker	202
Mayhem	203
Best Friends	205
Kimberly Sweeney	207
Relections of an Immigrant: First Years	209
Luz M. Whittenbarger	218
The Customer	219
New Home	221
Jacqui Worden	222
Photo Credits	223

Preface

Daiva Markelis

WE HOPE YOU ENJOY the essays, stories, and poems in *The Memory Pool: Reflections of Past~Forward*, the second volume of writing by the members of the Past~Forward memoir group. Our first book, *Occasional Writers: Bringing the Past Forward*, has generated a lot of interest and a gratifying number of sales. (You can order copies on Amazon.com.) Many of the themes from *Occasional Writers* reappear in *The Memory Pool*: the importance of family ties and the complexities of human relationships. There are more stories about childhood this time around, most of them funny, some wistful, even sad. And there are more glimpses into the distant past; a few of the stories are based on historical research and hark back to the Civil War.

Another addition is the 55-Word Story, a fairly new genre of writing; writers must use fifty-five words or fewer to capture the essence of a particular person, place, thing, or event. As the famed architect Mies van der Rohe has said, "Less is more."

The stories are often autobiographical and sometimes have surprise endings—this makes them even more fun to read.

The format of *The Memory Pool* is also slightly different from that of *Occasional Writers*. Entries are arranged in alphabetical order by the authors' last name; a brief biographical note appears after each author's contribution.

What remains the same is the enthusiasm Past~Forward writers have for sharing their memories and their willingness to be honest about often personal matters. If anything, the writing is even better in this second volume; one of the great pleasures of working with members of Past~Forward is to see their writing sharpen and mature. In addition, *The Memory Pool*, like *Occasional Writers,* is an almost entirely community effort. The writers reside in Charleston, Illinois, and surrounding areas; local artist Gaye Harrison designed the cover of the book; Cantraip Press, the publisher, is owned by local writer Mary Maddox.

We hope that reading the essays, stories, and poems in *The Memory Pool* will encourage you to consider joining the group, which meets twice a month. The afternoon meeting occurs the last Friday of the month from one to three o'clock in the Charleston Carnegie Public Library. Janet Messenger expertly leads the group—her patience, humor, encouragement, and expert organizational ability have enabled the group to flourish. The evening group meets the second Tuesday of the month from six to eight at Eastern Illinois University's Student Success Center. (We thank Kim Sweeney for finding this wonderful space.) I have the pleasure of leading the evening group.

The atmosphere in both groups is supportive and collegial: no topic is off-limits. In the process of reading aloud their personal narratives and poems, writers get a good sense of what works and what needs some revision. Members gently encourage each other to develop ideas and experiment with themes and styles.

There are no prerequisites, only an interest in writing memoirs. For more information, please feel free to contact Janet Messenger at jmess1@consolidated.net or Daiva Markelis at dmmarkelis@eiu.edu.

Daiva Markelis

ONE OF THE greatest joys of my life is leading the Past~Forward evening group. The writers are amazing—funny, poetic, moving, insightful, inspiring. I love them all! I teach in the English Department at Eastern Illinois University. My own memoir, *White Field, Black Sheep: A Lithuanian-American Life*, was published in 2010 by the University of Chicago Press.

Acknowledgements

Janet Messenger

The Past~Forward writers are grateful to all who contributed to the making and completion of *The Memory Pool: Reflections of Past~Forward*. Without their encouragement, inspiration, and support, this effort would not have been possible.

Thanks go out to Daiva Markelis, our mentor and friend, who has inspired and helped us develop our writing skills throughout the six years of Past~Forward's existence. Dr. Markelis is a creative writing professor in the English Department at Eastern Illinois University, a published author, and the editor of *The Memory Pool*.

Mary Maddox is the owner of Cantraip Press and author of the horror novel *Talion*. We thank Mary for her guidance, attention to detail, and assistance throughout the publishing process.

Gaye Harrison is responsible for the creative graphic design found on the cover and throughout the pages of *The Memory Pool*. She somehow managed to corral all the authors and capture the camaraderie we share as writers in the cover photo.

Thanks to Past~Forward's Publishing Committee, a.k.a. The Job

Squad: co-chairs Janet Messenger and Phyllis Bayles, and capable assistants Jane Gilbert, Dorothy Helland, Bill Heyduck, and Madi Ignazito. Any job that needed doing—they pitched in and got it done.

Thank you to the Coles County Arts Council, our sponsors, for their continued loyal support throughout the years.

We applaud Duke Bagger, Phyllis Bayles, and the Charleston Alley Theatre for writing and producing the very creative and lively program on November 2, 2014, at the public book-signing event for *The Memory Pool*.

Thank you to the Charleston Carnegie Public Library for providing monthly meeting space to the Past~Forward daytime group and arranging for larger public functions such as public readings and book signings.

We also thank Eastern Illinois University for providing meeting accommodations for the evening writing group's monthly meetings.

We appreciate Mr. William Warmoth's guidance.

And to our families and friends...you're the best!

Above the Beach

Phyllis Bayles

I was six years old and about as excited as a little girl could get—we were going to visit Aunt Chrissoula! Visiting Aunt Chrissoula meant a drive up to the big city of Chicago.

Dad wound the family Pontiac Star Chief along Lake Shore Drive, and my big brother Dean and I were thrilled with the wonder of sparkling Lake Michigan: all those boats in all those harbors and those big, tall buildings. We passed the magnificent white Bahai Temple and arrived in Wilmette, Illinois, a town of big homes and lots of rich people.

Our dear family friend owned a beach along Lake Shore Drive called Sand Lo Beach. It was a private haven for our family. On that first morning before we left for the beach, I watched as my mother took my new and beautiful swimsuit out of my little suitcase. My suit was bright yellow with pink ruffles that had white polka dots all over them. I even had matching sandals! They were yellow leather with pink silk ribbons that tied into bows over my toes.

We waved good-bye to Dad as he drove off for our hometown of

Danville. We were to stay with Aunt Chrissoula for the whole next week!

Every day of that week was summer heaven. Dean and I would trek down to the beach, meet our friends, and laugh and play all day long. Mother would follow with our baby brother, Little Art, and his assortment of diapers, bottles, towels, and rubber toys. At noon, we'd eat peanut butter and jelly sandwiches on a hill that had trees for shade. We'd sit on blankets and then, after eating, take naps. That was because mother believed you should never ever go swimming right after you eat. Mother would freeze water in milk cartons, so we had cool water to drink with lunch and all during the day when we got too hot.

We never gave Mother an argument when it was time to leave—we were hot and tired. Sometimes Theo Foti would pick us up in his big black Buick. Theo Foti didn't like other drivers very much and would often lose his temper. We heard he got so mad one time that he fastened a railroad tie to the front of his car and threatened to smash anything or anyone who made the terrible mistake of getting in his way!

I loved getting ready for my nighttime bath and seeing all that white skin next to all that brown skin. "Brown as a berry" is what Mother said about me. Every day I got browner and browner. Berry-er and berry-er. My hair got curlier and curlier—all that Lake Michigan water kept it pretty frizzy.

Dad returned the following Friday, and on Saturday morning we all went to the beach for the last time. After our sandwich lunch, Dad told me there was an ice cream parlor above the beach at the top of the hill. I didn't know that because we had never climbed up that hill. Daddy knew the owner because he was Greek; they both had gone to the same church. He gave me a dime and told me I could go up and get an ice cream cone. He said to be sure and tell Mr. Gus hello, and that his friend Chris would be up to see him shortly.

I skipped up the stairs that led up to the street and the ice cream parlor. All the way there, I tried to decide what type of ice cream I would get. Chocolate? Strawberry? My favorite was butter pecan—I wondered if they had that kind? At the top, I looked down to the beach and waved at my family—I felt like I was way high up. Even up as high as the clouds!

I pushed open the big glass door and was thrilled to see the huge soda fountain spanning the side of the bright white and blue store. There were painted pictures of Lake Michigan sailboats all over the walls and even a big boat where you could sit while you enjoyed a cone or a milkshake. What a place! I ran over to the boat and smiled at the people who were sitting in it. They looked away and didn't return my smiles or greeting.

Just then, a big, dark man with a mustache came toward me. He looked at the people and said, in a nasty way under his breath, "A mavro." I knew that word but didn't know why he said it. I looked around for the mavro. The man then pushed me and yelled "Get out!"

I cried all the way back down to the beach and ran into my daddy's arms. I told him what happened. I didn't understand. Had I misbehaved in some way? Why was that man mean to me? I didn't get to buy any ice cream!

Dad said, "Come with me." We went back up to what now was a place I feared. We walked in. The big man looked at my dad and shouted a hearty greeting. My dad pointed to me: "This is my daughter." The big man with the mustache looked shocked. Then Daddy and the man walked away. I never did know all of what was said. I did hear the man say words like "dark skin, curly hair, sway backed." When they finished their talk, the big man with the mustache presented me with a butter pecan ice cream cone. I remembered my manners and said thank you. Then we left.

As we walked down the wooden steps back to the beach, I could see my mother looking up at us with concern. When we joined her on the blanket, my dad told us that the man thought I was a *mavro*, the Greek word for black. And on that day, at six years old, my memories of sunny days at the beach had small clouds drifting into them. On that day, my dad remembered the unfairness of the slights against him when he immigrated to America. He never wanted his children to know that feeling, but on that day, I had my first lesson about intolerance.

On that day, when the clouds began to form, Daddy explained two new words to me — *racial prejudice*.

Presbyterian Surprise

Phyllis Bayles

The following story was told to Phyllis Bayles by her father-in-law, Dale Bayles.

Our friends Mary June and Roy Ogle always went to church with our family on Sunday. On this particular Sunday morning, we all headed up to the Presbyterian Church off the Charleston square.

Roy was a big cigarette smoker and craved a smoke before we went in. We sent the wives and kids on ahead. Then we took my little son, Mike, and strolled around the square. We took our time, looked into the storefront windows, and even sat for a spell on a bench. Roy smoked, and we enjoyed the lovely morning. Suddenly, we realized how much time had passed! We hurried back to the church and headed inside.

Services had ended and the sermon was just beginning. We stood at the back. We had no choice—we had to enter the sanctuary. We wanted to be invisible, but the only seats left were in a pew that was

The Memory Pool

way down in the very front. So, the three of us, as quietly as possible, headed down the aisle toward that front-row pew. We weren't exactly invisible. Lots of our friends turned to look, and some smiled and some waved.

Reverend Blair stopped speaking. It grew quiet. It grew silent. I'd say, almost tranquil. He looked at us. He waited. Everyone in church was looking at us. They waited. Believe me, we didn't even dare to look toward Elisabeth and Mary June.

We slid in and sat down. Then, trying to appear calm and sophisticated, we all leaned back to listen to the sermon. Reverend Blair gave us a saintly, yet what I would call somewhat devilish, smile.

WHAM! The big wooden pew flew over backwards, and we went over with it! Crash! With all the renovations going on in the church, the pew had not been bolted down yet!

I guess that's why nobody was sitting in it.

As for the minister, he just said, "I figured somebody would do that. I mighta known it would be YOU two!" When the whole congregation finally stopped laughing, he proceeded with his sermon.

A Nostalgic Passion

Phyllis Bayles

S HE WAS BEAUTIFUL. SHE beckoned you with tales of love and adventure. You could eat and drink with her and be amused at the same time. She welcomed the whole family inside. She got old and was slowly silenced. She clings to life. Can anyone save our hometown movie theater?

The Menu

Phyllis Bayles

The menu was a legacy of a hometown café. As an early form of guest communication, it was a memorable first impression. In some ways it needed to work nearly as hard as the staff did. It was essential to the welcoming, comforting feel of the environment in the Deluxe Restaurant in Danville, Illinois.

That one page, prepared on a mechanical typing machine and mimeographed in purple letters, had a true story behind it. It was the story of one man's fear, struggle, determination, luck, adversity, prejudice, loneliness, failure, and triumph. In a sense, it was a diploma, a certificate of great achievement, a proof of success.

The story began when my father immigrated to the United States in 1919 at the age of thirteen. My grandfather wanted to save him from conscription into the Turkish army. Papou took Daddy to the port and managed to get him onto a boat bound for America. Daddy was a child alone on that ship. His thoughts were a mixture of grief, longing, and fright. His dreams were nightmares of the cruelty of the Turkish invaders. As a child, my dad had been hidden when the

Turks entered his village. From his hiding place, he witnessed the rape of his grandmother and saw the invaders hang his grandfather. He prayed that he'd never again know such horror. Never again. In America, his father believed he would be safe.

Daddy eventually ended up in Wilmette, Illinois. He worked for an uncle in a restaurant as a busboy. After a long day at work, he'd take a 45-minute bus ride to English class at the YMCA. He learned to read and write English. He then learned mathematics. By the end of several years, he had the equivalent of an eighth-grade education. He learned history and became an American citizen. That was it for formal education. The rest he learned as he graduated from bus boy to waiter. His aunt and uncle, in an early version of home schooling, taught him American customs and manners. The cooks in the restaurant taught him their methods and recipes. Life taught him the remainder.

Years of struggle. Years of hard work. Years of tears and loneliness. He missed his family. He missed his home. Since most relatives were illiterate, and the mail service was often interrupted by war or corruption, it was difficult to stay in touch. Rarely could he share the joy of his accomplishments with anyone. The day he left his village, he never again heard his parents' voices. Here he had few relatives and fewer close friends. Daddy always relied on his Greek Orthodox faith for strength.

But all his efforts paid off! He learned the restaurant business, and in the early 1940's an uncle brought him to Danville as a trainee and potential future partner. He was handsome, hardworking, successful. He fell in love with Mother, a full-blooded Greek girl who was born and raised in the United States. He made the eleven-hour drive to Lansing, Michigan, five times to court her. She was educated. She was vivacious. She was perfect for him. When my grandfather insisted she answer Daddy's proposal, she stood up and said, "I say YES!"

Eventually he became a partner and then, after Papou retired, fully owned the Deluxe Restaurant. He found a new partner to help with the growing business. So, with an eighth-grade education, a pencil, an adding machine, and a manual mechanical typewriter, he ran his business. He became a success—good food was served to good people!

Daddy had a specialty dish. It was grilled halibut with homemade tartar sauce, a secret recipe. A group of men from McDonald's came in one day and asked for the tartar sauce recipe. Daddy wouldn't give it to them. Then, from her perch at the cash register, Mother saw them sneaking a bit of tartar into a vial to take with them for analysis. Evidently they failed because McDonald's tartar sauce isn't even close to tasting as delicious as Daddy's.

Is it a child's memory, or did food taste better back then? I think it really did taste better. I remember when the deliverymen came on a daily basis. Fresh bread and deep-dish pies from Arnholdt's Bakery, large boxes and burlap bags of Bredehoff and Ball produce from Jack Briggs, meat from Margolin's, halibut from Chicago, and assorted groceries, all delivered to the back door. In those days, there were no microwaves, nor were there big freezers. Everything had to be fresh and made that day. There was also real butter and real cream from the local dairy. Many businesses in town supplied the restaurant. Daddy helped keep them in business. Everyone worked together to be successful. Like Daddy, every single one of those men had a story.

The kitchen staff cleaned and chopped vegetables and fruit and also peeled potatoes. The potatoes were placed in a huge tub of cold water. The soaking removed the starch and make for superb fries and boiled, baked, or mashed potatoes. The waitresses cut the pies and placed them in the pie case. They took loaves of bread to their designated spots on the cutting boards. They filled tiny cream pitchers and sugar bowls and cut the butter into pats, placed exactly in the center of tiny porcelain plates. The cigar man came and replenished the boxes in the cigar display case. The candy man refilled the containers of Chuckles, boxes of other candy, and gum. Bill Kegley, our neighbor, delivered the large bags of freshly ground Superior coffee.

Dad's uncle, whom we called Papou, began making the daily homemade ice cream. It was always vanilla, chocolate, and one daily special like rum raisin, butter pecan, and strawberry. He would make a fresh sherbet from real fruit. With a meal, dessert choices were Jell-O, rice pudding, or ice cream. Over fifty-five years later, I find that most Greek restaurants carry the same three dessert choices.

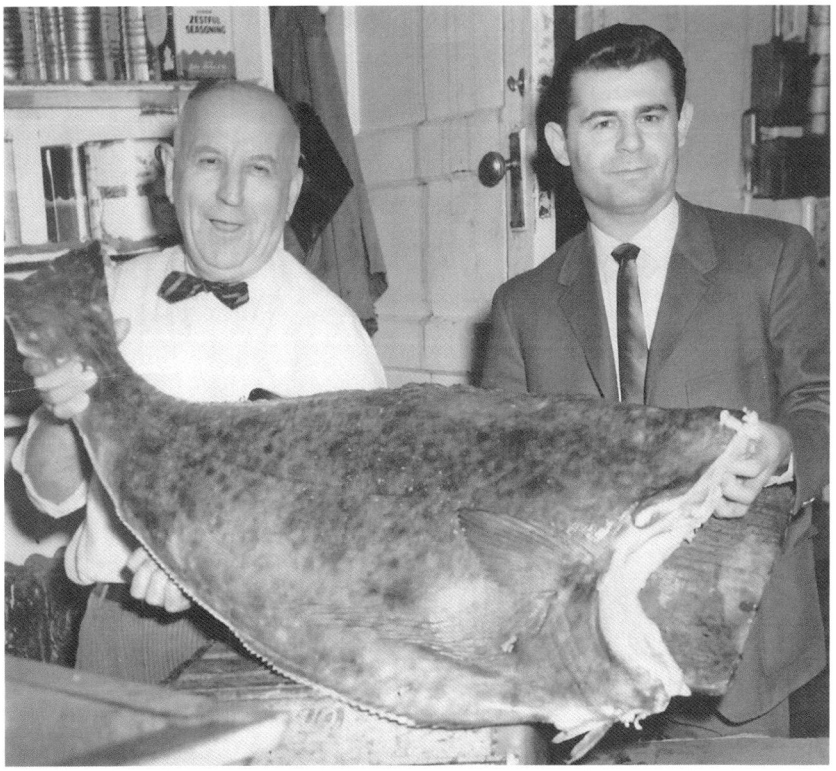

Model Star Laundry would deliver a huge pile of cleaned and pressed tablecloths and napkins. Each napkin had Deluxe Restaurant embroidered on its corner in Greek blue. On Saturdays and after school, I'd come by and make myself a chocolate milkshake. Then I'd sit at the counter and fold the linen napkins into the shape of crowns. I still know how to do that.

Each morning, the waitresses "dressed" all the tables with cloths and set out the white linen napkin crowns. The only paper in sight existed in the metal dispensers along the marble counters.

Daddy and a helper would go upstairs and haul the 200-pound halibut from a large claw-foot bathtub, where it had been submerged overnight in chunks of ice (from the iceman) and cold water. With his sharp knife, he expertly filletted and cut the fish into serving-size pieces. By closing time, all the fish would be gone, devoured by hungry customers.

While Daddy prepared the fish, the cook, Wardell, worked on the daily specials and supervised the kitchen help as they began the breakfast items.

Daddy would fill the cash register with the morning's supply of cash.

At six a.m. the doors opened and customers began streaming in. Many preferred to take a seat at the marble counter. Emma, the waitress, knew everyone's favorites but always asked, "The usual?" She knew where to place the ashtrays. She knew who drank their coffee black. She knew how they liked their toast buttered. Emma would squeeze the oranges for their juice. And she knew the customers' quirks. One customer liked orange juice on his cereal. Another put ketchup on his vanilla ice cream.

My father had the same greeting for everyone who walked in the door: "Fine day!"

He believed that every day was a blessing and, thus, every day was a Fine Day. Just about everyone in town knew that greeting and loved it.

One morning, Daddy got a call. The delivery truck had broken down and could not leave the Chicago distribution dock. The 200-pound halibut fish could not be delivered from Chicago—a crisis! The next day was Friday, the Deluxe's busiest day. Hundreds of customers would show up for halibut dinners and halibut sandwiches. They'd come with their families from surrounding farm communities. Friday night at the Deluxe was a tradition for many families. To deny them the most favored menu item was unthinkable.

With the determination that had followed him throughout his life, he knew what he had to do. Parked out back was his brand-new family Pontiac Star Chief. He started it up and headed for Chicago. The fish was packed in ice and loaded into the trunk. With lightning speed, he drove it back to Danville. He saved the day!

My brother came home from school later that day, and there was mother, pacing. She had The Look. You know, the one that says "I'm trying not to explode with anger." It was a tragedy of mythic Greek proportions. Mom's special luxury, the most expensive and precious new thing she ever owned, now smelled like 200 pounds of fish.

Every day at three o'clock, my father, Christ Bartges, sat down and created the menu that would be handed to each customer. He'd tap it out with two fingers on the typewriter, using the hunt-and-peck method. It was that menu that represented years of hard work and evidence of his success. It was that menu that paid for his family's college educations. It was that menu that showed he accomplished his objectives. It was just a simple, daily, low-quality piece of paper. But that one sheet of paper had a history behind it that no customer really knew. When I think back, it truly was almost a sacred document. It represented my dad's unbreakable spirit, his long, hard journey, and his desire to succeed with honor. It was his menu.

Phyllis Bayles

I GREW UP in Danville, Illinois, surrounded by a loving family of Greek heritage. There was Mother, Daddy, Dean, Art, Yiayia and Papou—all in one big two-story brick house on Franklin Street. My dear husband Eric ("Rick") and I met while students at Eastern Illinois University. He is the best thing that ever happened to me: my best friend and the reason my life has been laden with rich, beautiful, happy memories. I am blessed to have such a love.

For forty years we enjoyed successful careers in the Chicago area. Rick was an administrator in a northwest suburban school district with seven high schools, and I was an executive with a Fortune 200 corporation. When we retired, it was back "home" to Central Illinois and to Charleston, Illinois, a small Midwestern college town. There, I began writing the memoirs of my 98-year-old father-in-law, Dale Bayles. His memories of life, family, and career—spanning many decades—are warm, humorous, and colorful. I also began writing memoirs of my own life and experiences. Some I shared with family and friends, some I shared with Past~Forward. And some others, well, those I have kept to myself. That's because there are some experiences in life that are sad, heartbreaking, or joyous. These just reside in your heart, where they belong.

Memoir writers are the custodians of memories for future generations. Little did I know how meaningful these memoirs would become to family and friends. The preservation of these memories has created legacies that are priceless.

I urge our readers to take some time to remember events from your past.

People. Places. Good times. Sad times. What you heard. And what you lived. Your memoirs can be an act of healing. You can maybe unlock a mystery. You can spur readers to connect with your experiences.

And then, pick up your pen, or hit the keyboard, and bring the "past forward."

Singing to Fox
and Other Adventures on My Dead-end Road

Bob Clapp

Fox and his brother Gar would anxiously wait for our visits. They lived at the very end of our dead-end road. The dead end is long gone — today it's the smooth blacktop road that will take you out of Oakland north toward Newman. Back then, it was a gravel road ending next to Pierson's house on the east and Mary Ann's house on the west. She was the middle child of six siblings just like me, and both families shared a common poverty on the heels of the Great Depression and in the midst of World War II. Visiting Fox and Gar was inexpensive entertainment for two six-year-olds. Even better, all we had to do was sing a song and we'd earn a dime apiece.

To get to Fox's house, we had to go through a swinging gate at the end of the gravel road. The gate had a rope tied to it and to the fence around the corner. A weight was suspended in the middle of the rope. When someone pushed the gate open, the weight would rise and then pull the gate shut after you went through. I thought that ingenious.

We followed a worn footpath through the grassy pasture. The path led downhill to a small footbridge we danced across. There was water in the little creek bed only during the spring rains, but we looked for frogs and crawdads in the cattails and weeds. Going up the slope to the house, we came to another gate that was rigged like the first. Fox and Gar welcomed us into their old clapboard shack.

I'd look at Mary Ann for agreement at their request and we'd begin singing together:

You are my sunshine, my only sunshine,
You make me happy when skies are grey,
You'll never know dear, how much I love you,
Please don't take my sunshine away.

Fox and Gar would applaud our performance and hand us our dimes. We'd wave good-bye and hurry the 100 yards back to the road with visions of candy to be bought at Whistling Dickey's grocery store downtown on the square, six blocks away. A dime could buy more candy than our folks would appreciate us eating at one sitting, but they wouldn't find out about our purchase unless that nasty little bird that told Mom everything ratted on us. (Me and my brothers shot many a sparrow with our BB guns, as we figured they were the culprits Mom referred to when she often said, "A little bird told me.")

I can still see old Fox (his real name was Oliver Busby) as he strolled past our house on 610 North Walnut Street. I never knew him to have a car. He walked briskly for his overweight size. He always wore dark blue overalls and continually hunched his shoulders like he was trying to keep his galluses up. He kept his focus on the sidewalk in front of him as he peered through very thick but small round glasses. I don't know what he worked at, or if he even had a job or income, but I always knew he was good for a dime anytime Mary Ann and I had the courage to sing our favorite song for him and Gar.

All the families who lived on our dead-end street are gone now. More than half of the houses are gone as well, but new ones have been built to take their place. It's fun to return to the old neighborhood in my memory and recapture some of those good old days.

I sang "You Are My Sunshine" not only in duet with Mary Ann, but also solo as I swung back and forth on the rope swing in our next-door neighbor Keigley's backyard. I didn't get a dime for that, but I got a memory that is worth a lot more.

We had a jersey cow—I delivered milk and butter to some of the neighbors. One neighbor delivered a sound spanking to me and their grandson when we threw his sister's doll in the mow of the barn after stirring up a nest of bumblebees in the hay. The sister ended up in the hospital from the stings and we ended up with stinging bottoms—not only from the neighbor, but also from Mom when she got word about it. I don't think a little bird told her; I think Mr. Pierson told on us.

One of my favorite neighbors was Mr. Burtner. He also had lots of dimes to give away for neighbor kids who would help with his many chores. We pulled weeds from his garden, helped him shuck corn behind the wagon pulled by his two horses, and mowed his yard. We set spellbound as he told us stories while handing us fresh cracklings from the big iron pot where he rendered lard. Those hot cracklings were as tasty as any Baby Ruth candy bar.

Sadness permeated the neighborhood when word came that Charley's and Opal's youngest son was killed in the Pacific in the middle of the big war. But a few years later, everyone danced and shouted in the gravel street when the long war finally came to an end.

Life seemed a lot slower and safer in the early '40s. Once a week all the neighbor ladies gathered in Mom's kitchen for coffee, pastries, and lots of chatter. Something about that gathering made me feel good. I felt all of them not only looked after each other, but after all of us children in the neighborhood.

Thinking back, I remember upward of two dozen youngsters filling the dead-end road with antics. We knew there was approval from all our parents to discipline any of us children without respect to whom we "belonged." I think that made us feel safe, though maybe a bit more on guard. I wonder if folks today would feel uneasy if two six-year-olds wandered 100 yards from the old gravel road to entertain two old bachelors with their singing. Time brings lots of changes—some for the better, some not. One thing that hasn't changed is the good message in the song: "You are my sunshine, my only sunshine."

A Very Dark Day
in Charleston, Illinois, History

Bob Clapp

Based on a True Story

I'VE BEEN SITTING IN this old brick jailhouse for more than three months now. I am NOT guilty as they have charged. I had no intention of killing Nathan Ellington, my father-in-law. I simply acted in self-defense, and only after I had been attacked, badly bruised, and battered by his furious hand.

But of course no one in Charleston is going to believe me. I'm not a Charleston native like Nathan. My family, the Monroes, are well respected in the area—they're pioneers—but Nathan was greatly honored and loved. I'm just a stranger recently moved in from Falmouth, Kentucky. Nathan was a servant of the community as City and Circuit Clerk for two dozen years. It has been widely declared: "Nathan Ellington was one of the best men who ever lived in Charleston."

There was trouble between us since the day I started dating his daughter. Nathan's wife hated me from the beginning. Several disputes arose between the Ellington and Monroe families, and Nathan's wife encouraged the hatred she felt toward me in everyone who would listen to her, especially her husband.

I came to Charleston hoping to make a new life. I had such bright hopes. I seemed to fit right in as I started The Oyster Saloon. I also went into the drugstore business with Richard Norfolk on the west side of the square. I had friendly visits with many citizens at Collum's Tavern on the square's north side. I enjoyed fellowship with many of the notable citizens as we visited around the big open fireplace on cold winter nights.

How is it that fate has dealt me such a traumatic blow? True enough, I probably drank more liquor than I should have, but I was no stumbling drunk—I was a citizen in good standing. Sitting here in jail, I have written the following letter to my beloved wife:

> Dear Nannie, my sweet, my noble wife, what misfortunes have come upon us; what a cruel fate is ours, rudely torn asunder in the midst of joy and happiness, peace and love. (Alas! We loved too well for this world ... too well to last!) Oh, why should this sorrow have come upon us at such a time, when we were and could have been so happy together; when you had just proved your love to be as devoted as my own; when you had just proved your love and truth by clinging to me, even when discarded and disowned by your own relations for so doing. I never knew how happy I was until then, Nannie, for I never knew before how much you loved me. I never knew how inexpressibly dear you were to me, until I thought I had lost you; nor can you ever know, until you know it in a better world than this, how well I love you now. You are all the world to me; without you and our child, without you and your love, I do not wish to live.

Dr. Williams Chambers has gone to Governor Matteson and left word of my plight. But I'm not sure anything will come of it. There is such a stirring in the city against me. Time and again I've heard shouts from outside: "He ought to be hung today," "Let's bring him out and hang him," and "He doesn't deserve to live another day." I feel so little hope. Even Sheriff John R. Jeffries treats me like a dog. He brings me food and water, such as it is, but it's my wife and daughter who bring me moments of peace and hope. I am in the depths of despair most of the time. I have pretty much given up any hope that I will ever come out of this alive.

◆

In the community around Adolph Monroe, a desperate conspiracy had grown since the shooting of Nathan Ellington in October of 1855. Ellington supporters attended the trial under Judge Harlan and made frequent interruptions as they jeered and held up nooses to demonstrate their desire. After three days of deliberation, the harassed jury found him guilty and the intimidated judge went with the crowd and sentenced him to hang in thirty days, the middle of February of 1856. Meanwhile, Nancy and her mother-in-law wrote letters to the governor begging for mercy for the innocent man they believed Dolph to be.

On February 14th, the day before the scheduled hanging, a special messenger from the governor brought a letter to Sheriff Jeffries demanding a three-month delay so further investigation could be made. However, the supporters of Dolph were too quiet in contrast to the Ellington supporters, who were loud and boisterous. Scores of folks had come from miles around to share in a growing desire to see Dolph hang. A handful of instigators had stirred the growing crowd to take action. "Why wait for another trial? We know he is guilty. Are we gonna let him get by with this? He killed one of the most respectable men in town. Killed him in cold blood. He deserves to die — now — without any delay."

Each evening the crowd around the southwest corner of the Charleston square had been growing. On February 15th, the day Dolph was meant to hang, the fever of the crowd increased and the numbers grew to four or five thousand. The small brick jail on the square was surrounded.

About eleven in the morning, James T. Cunningham, Ellington's brother-in-law, stood before the crowd and informed them of Governor Matteson's decision. He further inflamed the crowd to "exert your-competence to handle your own affairs" without interference from the governor. Next, a man named McNary spoke against the accused and shouted they should take the SOB out and hang him now.

Someone began ringing the courthouse bell and the crowd seemed to take that as a signal as they all moved en masse toward the jail. A couple of fellows stepped out of the crowd and began taking hammers to the brick wall. Others began cheering them on, and when they got tired of swinging the destructive hammers, they handed them off to fresh hands. Adolph could hear the growing shouts and the pounding hammers.

After two hours, a hole was broken and the crowd increased its noisy cries. They quickly enlarged the hole, and one big fellow went in after Dolph. He gave no resistance. He was quiet and submissive to whatever fate awaited him as they dragged him through the opened hole.

The noise got louder as they led him to some nearby sugar maple trees, which they quickly decided were too small for a hanging. He was taken southwest to some much larger trees nearby.

As it became evident what was actually going to happen, the crowd began to get quiet with second thoughts. Apparently, many of them were coming to their senses. One or two even cried out, "This isn't right, we should let the law deal with him. Take him back to jail. Will you hang a dead man?"

This quieted the crowd even more and it seemed they just might back off from the nefarious deed. But some loudmouth shouted out of the crowd, "We all know he is guilty. We know he deserves to die. Hang the dirty SOB. Hang him now." No one seemed to have the courage to plead for the right of the prisoner and the supremacy of the law.

The crowd moved back, leaving a circle with seven men handling the prisoner. The silent, unresisting accused was lifted onto the waiting wagon below the noose. No one seemed to want to climb up and put the noose about his neck. A puppet of the unruly crowd was lifted to the wagon and ordered to put the noose on. Then it was just a matter of driving the wagon out from under him. It had become evident the crowd was divided on the matter. Many were ready to back off and give Dolph back to the wheels of justice. Others felt, "if we have come this far, we need to finish it." Someone only had to give the horse the "gid-up" and it would be done.

There were a few in the crowd who were not about to let this end without their own definition of justice. One fellow boldly stepped out of the crowd, yelling, "To hell with the courts, to hell with the governor. To hell with the wimps in this crowd." He gave the horse a smack on the rear and the wagon moved away, leaving Adolphous Monroe swinging in the air where he hung quietly without struggle to his death.

Charleston received the worst black mark on its reputation ever to be given the city. A few wept when they realized this had gone too far. Only a few cheered. The majority just silently turned and walked away with the realization that it never should have happened, and maybe they should have tried to prevent it. But now the deed was done, and future generations of the fair city would shake their heads in disbelief.

Adolph's wife Nancy, and his mother, sister, and brother-in-law fulfilled his last wishes that his body be taken back to his peaceful hometown in Kentucky and buried there. February 15th, 1865, will always be remembered as a black day in the history of Coles County and Charleston, Illinois.

The dark and ominous sky of that day seemed to underscore the tragic event.

Bob Clapp

BOB HAS BEEN a husband to Peggy for sixty years. They have 40-some grandkids, all living nearby, with whom they love to spend time. They enjoy life on 30-some acres of woods and trails just outside of Oakland where they have lived for forty-four years.

Bob is the author of *In My Steps*, a book he wrote in 2013 about his life with Jesus. Besides writing, Bob loves to make furniture in his workshop. He also loves to hike, canoe, kayak, camp, and catch big fish.

Besides attending two writing groups, he is active in two cancer support groups. He also enjoys preaching and teaching on the side. He survived a heart attack in 2012 and has battled stage four terminal cancer for four years. He often quotes his motto: "My goal is to live as long as I can, as strong as I can, and as far from any wrong as I can."

Bob is active in Rising Phoenix, a drug and alcohol Jesus-centered rehab organization based in Charleston, Illinois.

He is always available to speak about any of the activities in which he is involved. He can be reached at pneuma123@yahoo.com.

Wonderland Under

Lois Dickenson

I stared at the wooden door in the corner of the kitchen. Like the rest of the room, it was painted a creamy yellow, and the old-fashioned metal doorknob was just at chest height. This was a good time to try it, I thought. My sisters were arguing upstairs, brother was off doing mysterious boy things, and Mommy was putting the baby to bed. Supper was over — usually a noisy time — and the dishes were done. The kitchen was quiet and dim, with only the stove light on to hold off the night shadows.

I'd been through the door before, of course, but not very often. Mommy didn't like us kids going through that door alone. Too dangerous, she told us. That confused me a little, because I knew we went through the door to be safe from the really scary storms that bent and broke limbs off the old maple trees around the house.

I wanted to explore, but brother wasn't that interested, and my sisters didn't like it beyond the door. Besides, they were too noisy. They would insist on poking around and talking and explaining instead of letting me imagine new places and find new treasures. I wanted to do it by myself.

I turned the doorknob. It was a little loose, like all the doorknobs in our old house. It was dark beyond the door, darker than even the kitchen was. I didn't mind, although I was usually still a little scared of the dark. More important than the scary dark in my mind were the wonderful new smells beyond the door. The smell of rubber boots and wool jackets first, then laundry soap and vinegar, and then the heavier aroma of underground, musty and old, all overlaid by a fainter, cleaner scent that I didn't know.

I stepped down onto the landing and reached up to where I knew the light switch was by the door. Facing the down steps, I froze. I wasn't alone. Dim light shone through the open steps of the stairs and the lively sound of Louis Armstrong's trumpet played through the dimness. The music meant that Daddy was down there. Should I go down or back through the door? Daddy wasn't as likely to be as mad as Mommy at my coming down, especially as I wasn't really being naughty. And I knew Daddy liked to have me go in the barn or ride on the tractor with him sometimes. Okay, I decided, I was going down.

The steps were big ones for me, and the light was dim, so I went down like my baby sister did, one foot down and the other foot down beside it, one step at a time. I held on to the pole rail tightly. The steps were open at the back, but I knew nothing would grab my ankles because I had seen the wood cabinets filling the under-stairs space last time we were hiding from a storm.

Step down, step down, step down. I stopped several steps from the bottom. Looking up from my feet toward the light, I saw Daddy giving me a small smile.

"What're you doing, Punkin?"

I moved one shoulder a bit and looked down at my feet. It'll be back upstairs for sure, I thought.

"Come to keep me comp'ny?"

I nodded uncertainly.

"Okay."

I sat down on the step and peered under the railing. He sat on a high stool, under a bare dangling light bulb. The light bounced a thousand reflections off the canning jars that lined the wall behind him. Red, orange, green, they danced as the light bulb swayed. Between his knees, on a low table, a filled egg basket gently swished around in a tub of water. The vinegary smell of the disinfectant was strong and sharp. Off to the side of the table were the egg-packing crates. I knew about them, because Daddy had taken me along sometimes when he took them to the hatchery man in town.

We didn't talk. He continued to wash eggs, and I watched and listened to the music. Dixieland jazz changed to big band, Louis Armstrong to Glenn Miller. Daddy had taped long music shows off the radio to replay on his big tape player as he worked indoors like this. I liked to watch the big reels of tape move as the music played, but especially liked the zipping noise when the tapes moved fast backwards. We kids knew all the famous jazz and big band groups, and most of the musicals too, which was the music Mommy preferred. After a while, I edged down the rest of the stairs and began poking into the darker corners.

Here, on the other side of the stairway, was Mommy's washing machine. It was open at the top, with a mangle inside. Mommy had warned us all severely about staying away from it. We could lose a hand if we got stuck, she said, or burn ourselves in the hot water. I had seen the steam coming out of it one washday and believed her. On this side, too, was the tall white water heater—clearly another don't-touch item. I liked watching the flicker of the propane flame underneath it, though. It reminded me of the flame you had to light in the gas oven upstairs in the kitchen, where I was just starting to learn to bake things.

I had to take a big step over the drain in the middle of the room to reach the interesting section of cabinets on the far wall. The drain was interesting, too. Mommy used it on laundry day to drain the washing machine, which was not that exciting, but last year the basement had flooded after a heavy rain, and Daddy had to get a pump to help the drain get rid of the water. It was funny watching Daddy and brother stomp around in big boots, with the water halfway to brother's knees.

The cabinets had lots of interesting things inside. Laundry stuff, clothespins, strange bits of machinery, which went on the washing machine, I was pretty sure. Further along, there were tools, bits of wood and metal, and nails and screws. Another cabinet held boxes and jars.

"Don't touch those, Punkin. They're poison to get rid of the mice and ants. You'll get sick."

I shut the door quickly.

Just to the side of the cabinets, almost hidden by the shadows under the stairway, was another door opening. I'd seen it last time we had a storm and had wondered about it ever since. I'd asked brother what was in there, but he'd just shrugged and said "stuff." It was darker in there and I hesitated, but I could just see a big rumbling pillar beyond the door. Stepping closer, I could feel heat. The pillar had a small iron door with curlicues pressed on. The door had little slits in it, and light flickered behind them. It's on fire, like under the water heater, I thought.

"Don't touch the furnace, Punkin," Daddy called from the other room.

I stepped away. The furnace, I knew, blew hot air through the big grate in the floor upstairs. My sisters and I dried our hair over it in the winter. But we had to be careful about stepping on it, because it got too hot for bare feet sometimes. I definitely didn't want to touch the furnace where all that hot air came from.

Over in the far corner was another marvel. In the dim light of the well window, I could see a hanging sheet, hiding something. I stepped carefully over the floor, but there was no big drain in this room to trip me up. I touched the hanging sheet. It felt familiar, like the curtain around the bathtub upstairs. Peeking behind, I saw stacked boxes, but above…yes! There was a shower in the basement! I wondered why we never used it. With all five of us kids to get bathed, it seemed like Mommy could at least make my brother shower down here. He'd probably like it, too.

Peering through the grey light at the far corner, behind the rumbling furnace, I could just see a wooden wall with a big mound of stuff behind it. Moving closer, I realized this was the source of the smell I didn't know, faint and kind of earthy. I pulled myself up the wood wall, braced one foot in a crack in the boards, and peered over the top. Dark rocks, mounds and mounds of them. I frowned and thought. There were things my Daddy and Mommy and brother had said, things I had learned just this year in school. Coal, I thought, it must be coal. Coal burned, I knew, because I had seen it in my sister's Scholastic Weekly. I looked back. It must be for the furnace, I thought. I wonder how it got here? I needed to think about that some more before I asked somebody.

I wandered out to the stairs, climbed up a few and sat down. Daddy was holding each of the clean eggs up to the light bulb now. He was checking for cracks and to make sure there was no baby chicken inside. He had explained this to all us kids last year. It was very important that the eggs be clean and not cracked, he said, because they're going to the doctors to help make medicines. Remember when we took you kids to the school a while back and they gave you sugar cubes to eat? They grow that medicine in the eggs. I did remember the sugar cubes alright. It was the first time I had been in the school, the sugar cubes had been pink, and they had tasted kinda funny.

"You gonna sit with me awhile? " Daddy asked with a small smile. I nodded solemnly.

"Got your problems done?" he asked.

I nodded again uncertainly. I had just started arithmetic and wasn't always sure I did the problems right.

"Okay, then."

He held another egg up to the light bulb. "In the Mood" began to play on the scratchy tape. Daddy began to hum along. After a moment I began to hum along, too.

Testament

Lois Dickenson

The creek flowed past her feet, fast and brown with the runoff of days of rain. The little flat rocks—so handy as stepping-stones in dry spells—were lost under the surging current of the not-quite floodwaters. Poplars and cottonwoods rose over her, watching with sleepy eyes, just wakening in the not-yet spring. A gloaming sky and mist in the far woods circled round to meet the last flare of sun fire in the west.

Sunset, she thought. Perfect.

She reached down for the impromptu bouquet next to her on her shale slab seat. Hothouse flowers, of course, from the supermarket.

Sorry, sweetheart. It's all that's available this time of year. Forgive me?

She pulled the single white rose from the bundle, and brought it up to her lips. There was no scent, of course. Too bad, she thought. You always did love your gardens. All those years of pruning, mulching, and composting. I loved watching you plant new roses in our garden on Houston Street. She carefully plucked all the petals to hold them in her palm for a long moment, savoring old memories, then dropped them into the river current.

For all our years together, my dear. Loving, laughing, crying, hating. I'll remember it all, as no one else can now.

Three tiny pink tea roses came to her hand next. She cradled them softly, smiling and gentle, remembering. Tenderly she plucked the petals and scattered them into the wild water.

For Marcie, Jim, and Katie, our darling creations, our heart's blood. They're the best thing we ever did, aren't they? They made us so proud. I'm proud of us too, for keeping them close without smothering or fighting over them like some couples do. We did well.

Solemn now, she reached down into the grocery bag at her side and curled her fist around the small bundles of bitter greens, scavenged from the produce section at the supermarket. Laying them on the rock beside her, she reached back into the bag for the three small packets of pungent herbs. Using the empty bag as an impromptu bowl, she tore the greens into small shreds. Methodically, she shredded the chicory, kale, and collards, then sprinkled the cardamom, cumin, and celery seed over the whole thing. Closing the bag, she shook it, imitating all those salads tossed for family dinners through the years. Opening the bag, she flung handfuls of green memories into the rushing waters.

For all the pain and misery you caused me, all the embarrassment I endured when you... She stopped, glaring at the bits of green riding the wave tops. No, she thought, that's not right. It was time to be truly honest now with herself, and between life and memory. She took a deep breath and started again.

For all the pain and misery we caused each other, whatever the reasons may have been. The reasons hardly matter now, do they, to anyone but me? So let this bitter mix be for both of us, let them and the memories they represent be carried away to a place where they are not forgotten, but can do no more harm.

She sat on her rock for a while, as the light began to fade and the air to cool. The muted thunder of the water was soothing, easing the ache of memories.

Remembering is easy, but forgiving is very much harder—isn't it, my dear? Forgiving myself is even harder than forgiving you, I think. Of course, I haven't worked at it as long, so please be patient. She smiled a little. You were always more patient than I, though, weren't you? Don't worry, I'll get there sooner or later.

With a sigh, she reached down for the flower bouquet again. She picked up two lily blossoms—tiger lilies, the first she had seen at the market this year. Some people liked them to contrast with the white Easter lilies that were just now coming into season. She had chosen them, instead of the whites, just for their gaudy exuberance. She bent the stems, back and forth, back and forth, until they broke, leaving only the blossoms to be cradled in her palms. She smiled down at their orange-and-black splendor for a moment and tossed them into the water.

She watched as the blossoms rode the current, in line, following one another for a time, until the river eddies caught one and moved it into slower water, riding to the opposite side of the creek. Good, she thought, that's good.

For our lives apart, dear. For the pain and misery, which made us grow into paths we did not expect. For our new adventures, our new lives, where I found my Robbie, and, yes, you found your Carol. It turned out far better than I ever expected.

She watched the lily blossoms until they were carried around the river's bend. She looked up at the sky, still brightened by the sun's afterglow, but darkening rapidly in the east. Better finish this up, she thought. She reached down for the last of her bouquet, twigs of twisted willow.

So tricky to separate when I try to make flower arrangements at home, she thought. So fragile, and such a mess they make. I'm pretty sure they spray them with sticky stuff before they come into the stores, just so you can't buy just one or two sprigs. She frowned, momentarily annoyed with those unknown flower distributors. But then she smiled broadly, abruptly pleased with those pesky strangers, who had unknowingly provided her with a single, lovely tangled mass of curling twigs. Perfect, she thought.

Slowly she stood up and took a step forward toward the water. Her breath caught, and she stopped to squeeze and rub at her left hip. Darned arthritis, she thought, always making life more difficult. Another tentative step and she was at the water's edge. With a creak in her back, she bent over to launch the willow upon the river. Like a life raft, it floated and bobbed along, catching and carrying bits of debris away, down the current.

For us all, she thought. You, me, and the kids and grandkids, and all our old and new loves. For the family, for all our sorrows and joys, in the past and in the future to come.

She watched the little raft take the turn in the river to bob out of sight. She nodded, pleased with the outcome and herself. Slowly, she gathered the discarded stems and containers and pushed them into the crumpled grocery bag. Reaching down, she grasped her cane and walked slowly away, away from the river and its travelling memories, down the darkening forest path.

Lois Dickenson

I GREW UP as the middle child (of five) just outside Paris, Illinois. Being a farm kid, I spent a lot of my childhood outside: doing chores, climbing trees, floating leaf boats down ditches into mysterious culverts, fighting imaginary pirates holed up in our willow tree, building snow caves like Arctic explorers, or running from (imaginary) stampedes of wild pigs in our feed lot.

At age four, I got my first library card and immediately fell in love. The subject did not matter; if it was in a book, I read it. I studied history and philosophy/religion at Blackburn College and worked at several university libraries around the Midwest. I finally landed at Eastern Illinois University, where I specialized in government information and reference services, and materials preservation issues. While working at Eastern, I earned an MA in library science from the University of Illinois and continued to pick up graduate classes in history.

An amateur photographer and artist, I prefer abstract subjects. I use my history training to dabble in genealogy for family and friends. I knew I could write well from an early age—all that reading, I expect—and now realize the rhythm and line I respond to in abstract art carries over into my writing in the flow of a story and rhythm of words. I prefer to write fiction and poetry, for which I still credit—or blame—those imaginary pirates of my childhood.

A New World

Mary Dwiggins

When I was in seventh grade, I suddenly noticed there was a world of clothes I had not experienced. This awakening came from a TV show titled *Maya*. Though the show was a one-hit wonder of eighteen episodes that aired only one season, it was enough to turn me on to the first clothes I ever yearned after.

The TV series was set in the Indian jungle and centered on an American boy searching for his missing father. It starred teenaged Jay North (famous for playing Dennis the Menace as a child.) But the character I was most taken with was Raji, played by the very handsome fifteen-year-old Sajid Khan, whose sole purpose in life was to aid the American boy's search for his father in the Indian jungles with his trusty elephant sidekick, Maya. A typical American patriarchal story.

Most appealing to me, though, were not the wonderful stories, but the clothes Raji wore on all his adventures. His outfits were made of a crude material that I now know as khadi, a term for handspun and hand-woven cloth. In India, khadi is not just a cloth, it is a whole movement started by Mahatma Gandhi. But of course I didn't know all this at the time. I just knew it looked cool (as in groovy) and practical. After all, Raji could run, climb trees, and fight tigers in those outfits. And they were so versatile — he could "dress up" in these same clothes so he was presentable enough to be in the company of very important people. The one outfit that particularly caught my eye was a jacket designed in the style called Nehru. It was hip length, with a high-banded collar, and it fit tightly against his small chest. Now that was a jacket. I never did notice that both the Monkees and the Beatles had made them popular in the early '60s; I only knew that Sajid Khan was ever so beautiful in it. And I wanted one.

Now, in my family we rarely got anything any time of year except for Christmas and birthdays. My parents were practical that way. So in October, after the series started, I began hinting that I wanted a Nehru jacket for Christmas. I marked catalogs, taped a poster to my wall of Sajid Khan wearing a very nice green embroidered jacket, and I hounded my poor mother to death. There was no mistaking — I wanted it and I wanted it badly.

About this time, my best friend Sylvia brought another piece of clothing to my attention. Now, Sylvia was a wise girl, but sometimes she could say stuff that was way out there. This day, in particular, she really shook me.

We had just come from PE class and were walking together to our lockers when Sylvia turned to me with her most earnest expression.

"You know, Mary, it's about time you took a serious look at your body," she proclaimed.

"What?" I squeaked too loudly for being in a hallway filled with students. "Why do I need to seriously look at my body?" I was stunned.

"Well, you know how it is when you grow up. Your body starts to change."

"What's that supposed to mean?"

"Do I have to just come out and say it? Haven't you ever noticed that everyone wears a bra but you?"

"What?! How do you know I don't wear a bra?"

She was looking at me in a way that made me uncomfortable.

"Well, we do get dressed for PE," she said sarcastically. "Let's face it, you have more up there than Julia and she's been wearing a bra since last year."

I was mortified! My face reddened. What business was it of hers? Why was she looking at my body? And who else was looking at my body?! Oh my God! That was too much.

Well, needless to say, I had another item for my Christmas list.

That same day, my mom picked me up after school to take me to my piano lesson, so I knew I had her full attention while she was driving. In trepidation, I began my entreat.

"Hey, Mom," I started out slowly, "I really think I need some new clothes."

"Yes, I know," she said showing her irritation, "that new jacket. You know you'll have to wait for Christmas."

"Uh, no, something a little different," I said. I stumbled over my words. "I think I need a bra."

"A bra?" she said.

"Yeah, you know, a brassiere."

My mom was pretty quiet for a little while. I knew she wasn't quite ready for this. Heck, I wasn't either.

"Okay," she said finally, "let's look at the catalog when we get home. We'll see what we can find."

And she did what she said. When I got home from my piano lesson, sitting on the kitchen table was a National Bellas Hess catalog opened to the pages of intimate wear. We looked through the catalog together, I picked one out, and she ordered it. No big deal. It was that simple.

It took about two weeks, and, sure enough, in the mail came a medium-size cardboard box. My mom and the box were waiting for me at the kitchen table when I got off the school bus.

"Well," she said coyly, "I think you might have something in the mail."

She seemed a bit too excited about this bra business for my liking.

The first things my mom pulled out were two tiny, white, cotton starter bras. To be honest with you, that was all I needed. I was still quite flat.

She handed them to me and I held one of them up. "Not much to it," I said.

"Oh," she said as if she were surprised. "There's something else." She had a strange look on her face. A half smile, and her eyes were shiny. She then slowly pulled out another package and handed it to me.

"What's this?" I asked.

"Just open it," she said in a whisper.

The heavy brown paper bag crinkled in my hand as I tore off the tape that held it shut. I reached inside and pulled out a bundle of hunter green corduroy material. Unfolding it, I suddenly realized that, in my hands, was my coveted Nehru jacket with matching bell-bottom pants. Words cannot express the joy I felt to be the owner of a new Nehru pant set. I was elated! I was speechless.

"Thanks, Mom, for the jacket," I finally eked out the words. "Oh… oh yeah…and the bras." I reached across the table and we hugged. Releasing me, she gazed deeply into my face. She looked at me differently in some way.

"But it's not Christmas," I joked, breaking the moment.

"Well," my mom pronounced emphatically, "Sometimes a young lady just needs a little something now."

I loved that outfit. And it represented a special bonding moment between me and my mom. Not only did I never notice that jacket wasn't khadi, I also never realized that, thanks to my new bras, it didn't fit quite the same way on me as it did on flat-chested Sajid Khan.

sajid khan
dream
someday
EXCLUSIVE
OFFICIAL BRITISH
BEATLES BOOK
SURPRISE WINNER!
TEEN DATE book
SAJID!
SAJID TAKES YOU HOME
MARK: "HOW TO ATTRACT ME"
DAVY: "MY LAST DAY ON MONKEE SET"
FIRST PREVIEW! MONKEE MOVIE
COWSILLS: EUROPEAN TOUR
MONKEE SECRET DIARY
16 MAGAZINE
100 HUSH-HUSH PIX! SHOCKING TRUE STORY
10 COLOR CALORE!
SAJID
BOONE
COWSILLS
RAIDERS
STAR TREK

Keeping Time

Mary Dwiggins

THE ROOM IS DARK and I can't see a thing, but my bladder says it's around five a.m. Lifting my stiff body off the bed, I slowly make my way to the bathroom and flip on the light. The clock on the shelf behind the toilet flashes 5:07.

"Yep," I say quietly to the bright numbers, "just like clockwork. That pesky bladder just won't let me sleep more." The time change is no friend to my body. It knows it should be 6:00.

I do my business, then fill a cup with water from the sink and take a pill out of a bottle that sits just to the left of the toothpaste. I shut off the lights.

I make my way back to bed feeling along the wall and dresser as a guide. The room seems darker. My eyes had gotten used to the bathroom light so they won't remotely see anything now. When I reach my bed, I place the pill and cup next to the clock that sits on my nightstand.

"Did you take your pill?" my husband asks, waking up slightly.

"No, it's not time yet," I say in a whisper. "Go back to sleep."

Mark groans something I can't understand. But, soon enough, I hear the deep rhythm of his breathing that indicates he is asleep again.

I periodically push the little button on my alarm clock to illuminate the numbers. First it reads 5:26, then 5:38, then 5:49.

Finally the clock reads 5:55. I love it when I see all the numbers on a clock the same. It seems like good luck when that happens. I am glad it can never say 6:66. "I love time," I say to myself. I shut off the alarm before it goes off, then reach over and take my pill. I wait for the levodopa to kick in before I get up so my body isn't so shaky.

Mark's alarm goes off and I know it's 6:15. His clock says 6:26, but he isn't duped into thinking it's right because he goes back to sleep for ten more minutes.

Why do people do that? I think.

At 6:30 my time and 6:41 his, we get up and dress for our day, then make our way to the kitchen.

"When do you walk with Amy?" he asks, looking at his wristwatch.

"Later than usual. Not till eight o'clock."

The clock on the stove says 7:00 and I can eat now. I have to wait an hour after taking my pill. Breakfast is two fried eggs, toast, and juice.

"Too bad we won't get to have as many eggs this winter," I say to Mark as I hand him his breakfast.

I raise chickens. I have five of them and I'd been getting four to five eggs every day. Young chickens lay eggs consistently, for the most part, starting at around five months old. This will continue until they molt their feathers at around two. Production will dwindle to three or four eggs per week after this. The chickens we raised are two years old now, so production has slowed down. The biological time clock of chickens. They say, whoever they are, that the eggs become much richer when this happens. And I believe this is true in our case. But time is money. Egg farmers usually sell their chickens to soup companies when their chickens turn two and start over with young ones so they can keep profit margins steady. I know this. But that's not an

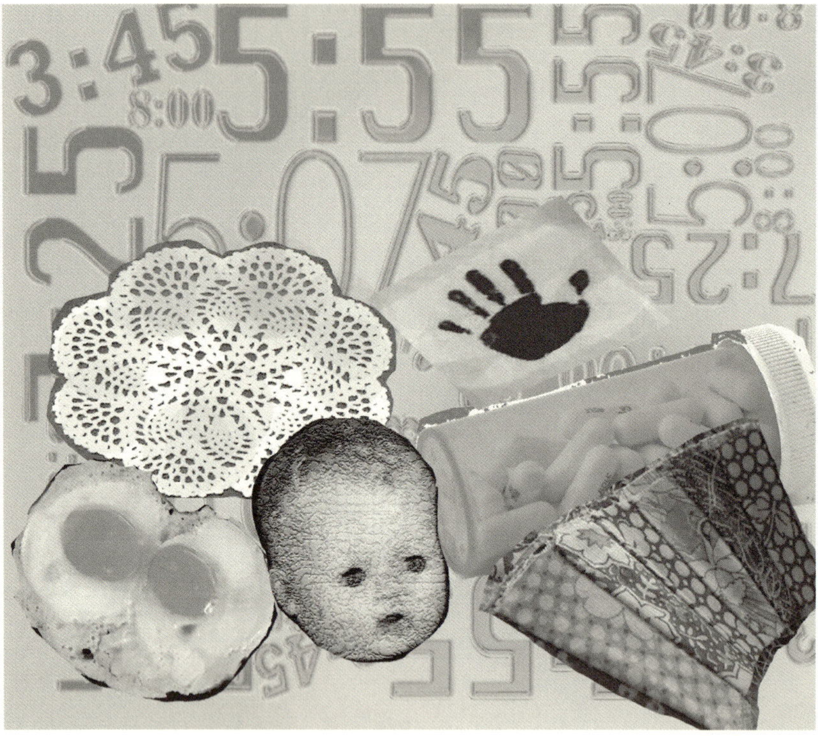
3:45
8:00
5:55

option for my girls. They will live out their lives here on our property even when they are no longer laying. But I know their time is short.

Mark eats his breakfast and savors every morsel that enters his mouth. I love that about him, that he enjoys every aspect of his breakfast. But as usual he takes too much time with this. He suddenly looks up at the clock on the buffet in front of him. The hands say 3:45 from a long-ago time. It startles him as usual.

Quickly looking over his shoulder at the wall clock by the refrigerator he sees the real time is 7:25. "I wish that clock kept time better," he says.

"Clocks keeping time. What a lie," I say. "Nothing keeps time."

"You do," he says smiling. "Look at the family tree you painted downstairs. And your mother's hope chest."

Do I really keep time? I think about all the sayings about time and how they apply to me. I did have a beautiful mural of a tree painted on the wall in our family room where I hung pictures of our parents, their parents and on back to five generations. I have these pictures because somehow I have been deemed the historian for a family who wants to get rid of their old pictures. "You are the keeper of our story," my brother once said to me. But am I a keeper of time?

I love opening my mom's hope chest. It's like visiting her. It has evolved through the years since she gave it to me umpteen years ago. When I first got it, it contained the stuff my mom held dear. Lots of stuff. Her grandmother's quilt pieces, her mother's handmade doilies, an old doll that she got when she was nine. The doll's hair has come out in clumps, the hard shell of the head cracked into thousands of lines. It scared my daughter Maggie the first time I got it out to look at it.

Since my mom's death, I have thrown away a few of the things damaged by the passing of time, a new meaning to the phrase "time wearing thin," and I've added my own treasures to the chest. Time-cherished things like my children's baptismal gowns, pictures of handprints and drawings made at various stages of their lives, Maggie's Easter dress my mom paid more than sixty dollars for back in the day when she could least afford it and that price was unreasonable. I may go back in time for a fleeting moment. But am I a keeper of time? I wish I were. I would hoard it up and dole it out in small chunks for myself and the people who need it so much. Maybe it's more like I preserve time.

My doctor has told me that my faithful walking eight to ten thousand steps a day has kept my Parkinson's from progressing more quickly. He has also given me a pamphlet telling me ways that I may borrow more time. So I know I am a borrower of time and I am so desperately thankful for the time I've borrowed.

I also know that I can kill time. That's what I will do as soon as Mark leaves for work and I have to wait until it's time to pick up Amy at eight. But keeping time? I can't keep time any more than a clock can keep time. I wish I could. One thing I do know, whether I have a lot of time or not: I sure can spend it.

Mary Dwiggins

Mary Dwiggins moved around a lot until she was ten years old, when her stepfather quit the Air Force and moved the family to a farm in Macon County, Illinois—"out in the middle of nowhere." Many of her stories reflect how she, her brother, and her mother coped with the many transitions.

Fleeing with all possible speed at the age of eighteen, Mary went on to earn her BA and MA in English at Eastern Illinois University. Her career has taken her many places including back to Eastern Illinois University and Millikin University, where she taught many classes including children's literature, hypertext novels, and freshman writing.

She is currently researching local stories involving the Orphan Train and Broomcorn Johnnies, which will be incorporated into a young adult novel. She enjoys gardening, writing, and "hanging out" with her husband and three grown children. She is looking forward to her upcoming retirement where she believes she will devote her time to her most important work, writing full time.

She is a member of the Past~Forward memoir-writing group. "We are the story-keepers," she says about the members of the writing group. "We create heirloom memoirs and I am confident that someday our families will be grateful for the stories." Three of her memoirs, *New Stepfather*, *Meeting Grandma*, and *How to Shrink a Head; or Being a Trophy Wife Sucks*, have been performed at the Charleston Alley Theatre. Ms. Dwiggins resides in Charleston, Illinois.

The Civil War
and My Ancestors

Hannah Eads

To get away from the turmoil of the Civil War, my great-grandparents moved from Jonesborough, Tennessee, to a farm in Edgar County, Illinois, in the 1860s. John Riley Smith paid $1,000 for a substitute to fight in his place in the Confederate Army. He had married Margaret Christina Andis in 1849.

Margaret Christina was my mother's grandmother, the youngest of nine children born to John and Nellie Andis of Abingdon, Virginia. Margaret's parents died when she was young, so she went to live with her older sister, Polly, who was married to Jacob Lynch. He was elected Clerk of the Court, holding office for many years in Abingdon.

Margaret Christina was educated at the Martha Washington College in Abingdon, where Jacob Lynch was a trustee. She became a schoolteacher after graduating. The college was used as a hospital during the Civil War. Major Jacob Lynch fell ill with pneumonia while he assisted in the burial of Confederate soldiers and died in 1862. The school is now The Martha Washington Inn.

The Civil War must have affected the family greatly. In his book, *Reminiscences of an Old Timer*, my ancestor, Captain Ross Smith, gives a firsthand account of life in Jonesborough during the Civil War. The following passage is quoted from his book:

> Along between the years of 1856 and 1860 James Buchanan was our President. I went to school and helped on the farm. We kept a few sheep, sheared them, hauled wool to a carding machine, where it was made into rolls which my mother would spin into yarn for our clothes…As the War progressed times grew harder. It was pretty tough to make ends meet. I would have to go eight or ten miles to a country mill for flour and bring it home on horseback. Then groceries became very scarce. For coffee we parched wheat, or cut sweet potatoes into small cubes and parched them. If our tallow dips gave out for a light at night, we would take a rag and lay it in a saucer of fried grease. There was no coal until after the war ceased.
>
> Finally the Confederate forces lost control of Upper East Tennessee, and then it was that small parties of both Confederate and Federal Cavalry rushed back and forth between the two armies. What one left, the others took. They robbed our field of what little corn we had raised and at last stole our horses, leaving us without any means of making a crop of any kind.
>
> But all of these degradations must not be laid to either force. These actions were confined to forage for food. There were many men laying out in the mountains to keep out of the army, and they often made a raid in the valley for provisions.

Margaret Christina's family was involved in both sides of the Civil War. Her brother, William Andis, enlisted in the Virginia 64th Infantry Regiment as a private in the Confederate Army. William's son, Earl

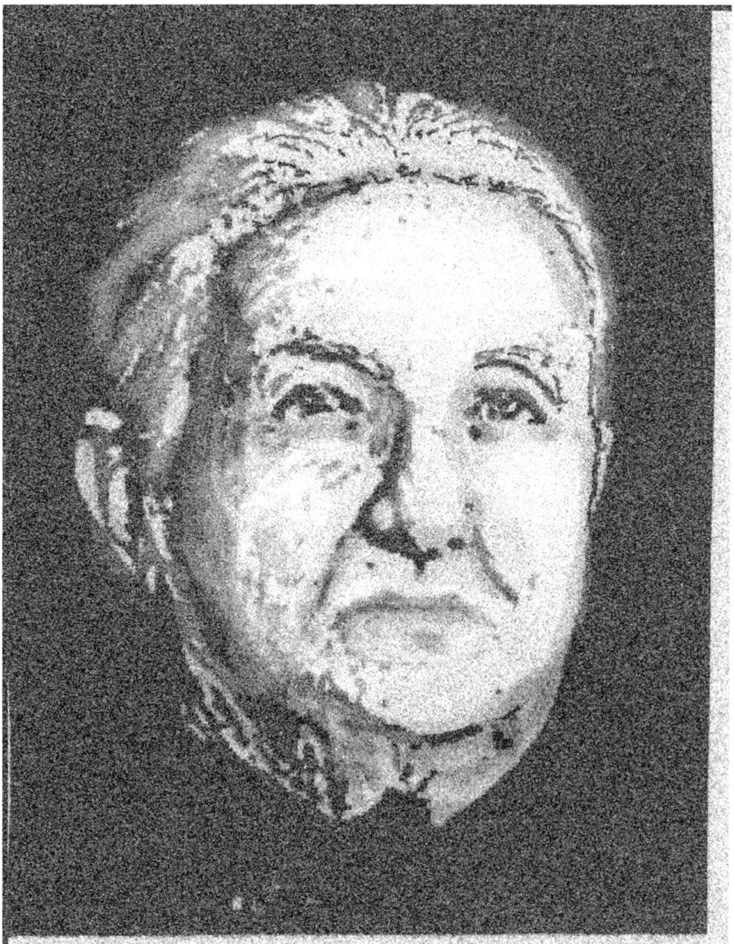

Carson Andis, enlisted as a corporal in the Confederate Army, and was promoted in 1863 to full 1st lieutenant. Another brother, Alexander Andis, was an early pioneer in Indiana and served in the Indiana Cavalry from 1862 to 1865, as noted in the Soldiers Discharge Record, Recorder's Office, Greenfield, Indiana. Yet another brother, John Andis, Jr., was reported to have died in the Soldiers' Home in Washington, DC and was buried in the National Cemetery in Arlington, Virginia in 1862.

A sister, Jane Andis, who married Henry Smith, had settled in Indiana. Henry Smith was in the Civil War Draft Registration for Brandywine, Hancock County, Indiana. It's not known if he served in the war. Another sister, Sarah Ann "Sallie" Andis, was the wife of Samuel Montgomery Hale, who enlisted as a private in Company F, Virginia 45th Regiment in the Confederate Army. Yet another sister, Eleanor "Ellen" Andis, was the wife of Williamson Carter, who served in the Civil War in the Virginia Cavalry. He enlisted in 1864, and fought for the Confederacy. He went AWOL in 1864, and was paroled in 1865. Eventually he received Distinguished Service status, according to records.

A cousin, Margaret Ellen Andis, became the wife of Colonel John Calhoun Dickenson after his first wife died. Colonel Dickenson wrote an autobiography in which he described the disastrous effects of the war upon his property, noting that he never received payment for the Confederate Army "taking 17 good horses, 98 head of fine cattle, 200 fine sheep and about 4,000 pounds of bacon...I also lost about 40 likely Negroes by Lincoln's free proclamation and valuable tracts of land that were paid for in Confederate funds."

Margaret Christina Andis Smith's newspaper obituary is titled "Another Pioneer Resident Gone." It states that she departed this life Oct. 20, 1914, aged 86 years, 7 months, and 5 days. Her husband, John Riley Smith, died April 1, 1908, age 83 years, 8 months, 16 days. Both are buried in the Embarrass Cemetery, Edgar County, Illinois.

My Mother

Hannah Eads

It was after midnight, and my mother's room at the nursing home was dark except for a faint yellow light coming into the room from the hallway. She was in a deep sleep, and the nurse who had summoned me earlier came into the room asking if I would like for her to bring in some oxygen to help my mother's shallow breathing. The nurse appeared a moment later with a canister on wheels and inserted the oxygen tube into my mother's nose. "She'll not last the night," the doctor had said. Mom passed away as I held her small, bony hand.

It was only the week before that we had a family gathering at the nursing home to celebrate Mom's birthday. She was 102 years old on the first day of August 1999. My brother, Richard, had predicted that we would be getting together again soon for a funeral because Mom's health was failing fast and she slept most of the time.

Mom liked to tell stories about her childhood. When she was born in 1897, the automobile had not yet been invented. She called her father "a rolling stone" because he moved the family often — he held a degree in optometry, but never practiced. He moved the family to a farm near Borton, where he operated the telegraph. Mom said they had an oil well on their farm—the pigs wallowed in the oil. About that time, both of Mom's parents became ill with typhoid fever. Times were bad, and they lost the family farm because they couldn't pay the taxes. Her parents sent Mom to live with her first cousin, Ferne Chesrown, while they recuperated.

It was on the Chesrown farm that Mom learned to ride a horse. The horse was startled by a snake and threw her off when she rode down the lane to get the mail. She never rode the horse after that. The farm was close to Catfish School, a one-room country school located on

Catfish Creek. Mom told a story about her teacher, who was walking home after school in the winter. A sudden blizzard came and the teacher froze to death.

Mom's dad then moved the family to Brocton where he ran a hotel. One day some gypsies came into the hotel to tell her mother's fortune. When they left, her mother's gold jewelry was missing. Her dad also ran a grocery store, but had to close it because too many people bought on credit and couldn't pay him what they owed. She recalled that the family went to the Methodist Church in Brocton every Sunday and that her three brothers would escape from their Sunday school classroom by crawling out the window without their parents ever finding out about it.

When Mom was still a little girl, her father moved the family to Monteagle, Tennessee, high up in the mountains, because he thought that the altitude there would be good for his health. Mom said that her only playmate was the little "nigger" girl, as she called her, who came with her mother to do the laundry. Mom lamented that they moved so often that my grandmother Hannah's paintings were left behind.

After living in Tennessee, the family moved back to Brocton, where her father ran a "bucket shop," which was something like betting on the market. He made a lot of money then and bought Mom a $500 pearl necklace. He bought one of the first automobiles, a Reo, which my mother learned to drive. But she had to have one of the men crank the motor because the crank was too difficult for her to turn. Roads were beginning to be built at that time although most in the area were still dirt roads. Electric cars also made their appearance; a lady in Paris, Illinois, owned one.

One mystery about Mom that may never be solved is why there is a photograph of her dressed in a World War I uniform. The only clue is that she mentioned going with her best friend, Eutha Allen, to the train station to wave at the troops as they passed by on the trains. I don't know of any of my ancestors who served in World War

I. Perhaps Mom had a friend who was a soldier, or maybe her friend had a brother or friend who was in the service.

Then, in 1917, Mom and Eutha Allen rode the interurban from Brocton to Mattoon to see the devastation created by the infamous tornado that ripped through Mattoon and Charleston.

Mom was a small, 5-foot-2 woman with blue eyes and freckles, which she blamed on her Scotch-Irish ancestors. She had long brown hair that she always wound into a bun at the nape of her neck, held in place with hairpins. She never wore make-up, and usually wore an apron over her dress. I have vivid memories of Mom hoeing in her huge garden wearing a sunbonnet she sewed out of cotton fabric using a pattern handed down to her from her mother.

We ate tomatoes, lettuce, green onions, carrots, peas, green beans, and potatoes fresh from the garden. Mom canned green beans and tomatoes to eat in the winter. She made sauerkraut in a big round crock, putting a big rock on top as a lid. She raised chickens, and my dad ate lots of fried eggs and fried potatoes. We had fried chicken every Sunday, but my favorites were Mom's bean-and-ham soup with cornbread and her grape pie made with purple grapes from our grape arbor.

Mom made lye soap to use in the laundry using leftover grease saved from cooking. She put the grease and other ingredients into a huge iron pot and cooked the mixture. After it cooled, she cut it into bars of soap. She also made use of some folk remedies just like her mother had done. Every spring, she would burn a yellow lump of sulfur on the big iron stove to purify the stale winter air. She would gather the first tender young dandelion greens of the season and boil them because she claimed that eating them would purify the blood. Another remedy was sassafras tea. Mom would boil the sassafras roots to make the pink tea. Ginger tea, with its spicy fragrance, was her cure for indigestion. A folk remedy of which I was the recipient was a cloth-wrapped baked onion poultice for my earaches. I had to

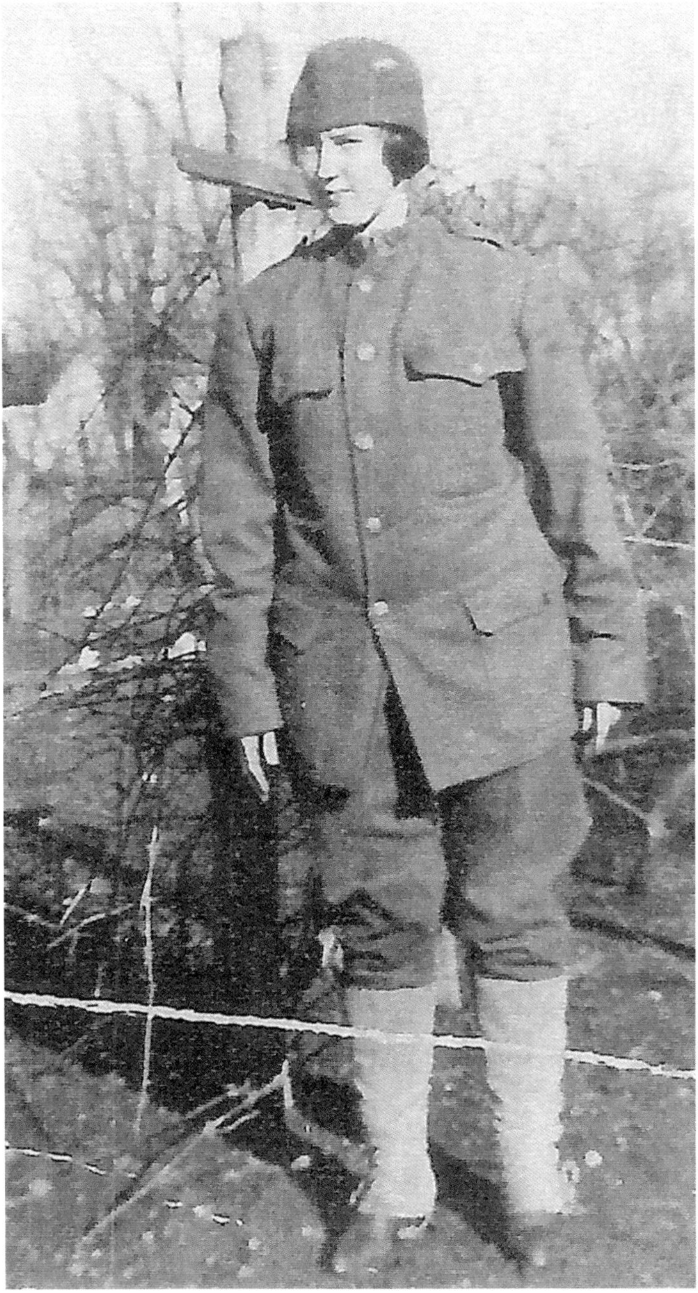

sit and hold it on my aching ear, and the warmth made my ear feel better. In addition, my two brothers and I would have to swallow a spoonful of cod-liver oil several times in the winter because Mom claimed that it was good for us.

After she passed away, we found a scrap of paper in her Bible on which she had written her epitaph: "My family was the most important thing in my life." We gave this note to the pastor to read at her funeral, which was held at graveside, with friends and family gathered around the tent on a bright, sun-lit morning in August. A blanket of Mom's favorite roses and summer flowers covered her casket, just as she would have wanted.

Hannah Eads

My childhood was spent growing up in Paris, Illinois. Ever since I can remember, I've wanted to be an artist. When I graduated from Paris High School, I received a four-year scholarship to Eastern Illinois State Teachers' College, where I majored in art. I received a BA and MA in art from Eastern Illinois University, and a doctorate in art education from Illinois State University. I married, had two children—Mark and Michelle—and then divorced.

While at EIU, I established the Summer Art Camp and the annual Art Education Conference. I was honored with the EIU Outstanding Teaching Award as well as the Illinois Art Education Award for long-standing contribution to art education. In 1991, I retired from my position as Professor of Art at EIU. Through the years, I exhibited my paintings in competitions and won several awards. My paintings are represented in private, university, and corporate collections.

After retirement, I traveled the world, painted with watercolors, and, with the encouragement of the memoir group, began writing memories of my childhood as well as stories about my travels. When my cousin traced our Milburn lineage back to 1600s England, I became hooked on genealogy. Since that time, I've been researching my Newgent and Smith family histories, and have donated copies to the Charleston Public Library and the Edgar County Genealogical Library. But names and dates aren't interesting without the family stories that have been passed down from generation to generation, so I'll continue writing.

La Grange Park

Marty Gabriel

When I was seven years old my family moved from a two-flat apartment in the Austin neighborhood on the west side of Chicago about ten miles away to an old farmhouse on the outer edge of La Grange Park. After having moved from one apartment building to another in the city, I welcomed the opportunity to live in a quasi-rural area on the two acres of land that my folks had purchased. The landlord at our previous residence had forbidden my brother and me from playing on "his sidewalk" firmly enough that I heeded his edict even though my parents assured me the city had actually constructed the sidewalk for public use. Playing on the tiny lawn in front of the landlord's building, of course, was definitely prohibited.

But while I was very glad to be in this wonderful new playland, I still felt somewhat strangely disconnected. I remember hearing that we lived in an "unincorporated" area and I assumed this meant that we were really townless and adrift in some way. I saw myself then, as I reflexively tend to do today, as an earnest and ethical but essen-

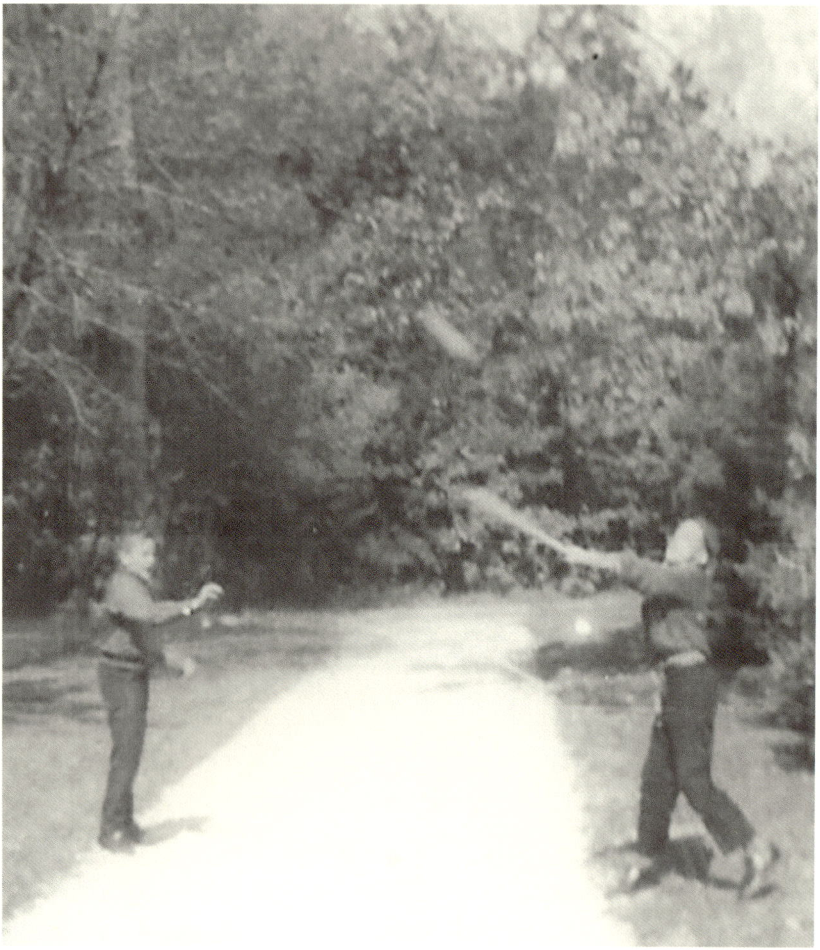

tially interloping outsider.

La Grange Park is next to La Grange, which literally means "the farm." However, by 1959 farmhouses could no longer be found in the vicinity of either suburb, except for ours and those of our immediate neighbors. Our front acre included not only our farmhouse but also a stable, a toolshed and a large, gravel, horseshoe-shaped driveway. It also had a huge black maple, towering oaks, crabapple trees, a tulip tree, a weeping willow, and various other trees, shrubs, flowerbeds, and gardens. One of our neighbors had horses. They escaped their enclosure and ran joyfully around our property a few times, alternately scaring and amusing me. Another, older, neighbor had a huge tractor mower and he kindly used it to help us maintain the condition of our clear-cut back acre, which we soon turned into the unofficial neighborhood ballfield, complete with a sturdy backstop my father built from two-by-fours, plywood, and chicken wire.

Weather permitting, my brother and I would make the four-mile round trip from our farmhouse to the Forest Road Elementary School on our bicycles. The first half-mile was quite bumpy, as the road was first gravelly and then an uneven mix of blacktop and potholes and stones, but soon enough we'd reach what apparently was the "incorporated" area. The Robinhood Ranch subdivision consisted of block after block of well-manicured, two- and three-bedroom, brick, ranch-style homes on single lots, but all that mattered to me were its streets, its beautifully smooth streets. "The streets, the streets, paved with concrete," I'd sing happily upon our arrival.

There weren't as many trees in Robinhood Ranch as one might have suspected, and there were even fewer in Sherwood Village, another expansive subdivision adjacent to Robinhood Ranch. Similarly, Forest Road School was not in a wooded area as its name implied. Instead it was surrounded on all sides by slightly older versions of Robinhood Ranch and Sherwood Village. Nonetheless, I had a special feeling about the name of the school because, unlike my classmates, I actually lived on a road by a forest.

From the picture window of our farmhouse I could look across the front yard past the old white well-water pump in front of the row of gigantic sweet-smelling lilacs that grew above the ditch on our side of the gravel access road—there, just on the other side of the road, was Brezina Woods. Our mailbox was located more than a half mile from our home just outside the front entrance of the Brezina Woods Forest Preserve. It was on Mannheim Road, which is part of Rt. 45, alternately a rural highway and city thoroughfare that runs the length of the country from the Ottawa National Forest on the Michigan peninsula near Lake Superior to Mobile, Alabama, by the Gulf of Mexico. To get to our mailbox or to the homes of our closest relatives or to the Jewel food store or to the Eden Lanes bowling alley, we would travel from the rear entrance of the forest preserve near our house, through woods and picnic grounds to Mannheim Road.

After I got my eyeglasses I enjoyed looking out the windows during our frequent trips through the woods. I was especially drawn to a particular stretch of Mannheim/Rt. 45 near our mailbox. The road, which crossed over a bridge that spanned Salt Creek a little north of our mailbox, was closely flanked there on each side by tall oaks. It was fairly easy to see Salt Creek meandering along one side of it, thirty to fifty feet below the level of the road, as we headed south away from the bridge on our return home.

I always felt compelled to look at the creek, and I did so with a mixture of curiosity, awe, and fear despite a recurring nightmare in which I would lose control of a car I was driving south on Mannheim past the most precipitous drop. Regardless of whether I was driving quickly or cautiously, the car appeared to have a mind of its own and it would suddenly veer off course for no apparent reason. With my nose pressed to the windshield, I would find myself hurtling headlong toward the creek, gaining momentum that I was powerless to stop. I always awakened breathlessly, heart pounding, an instant before hitting the water.

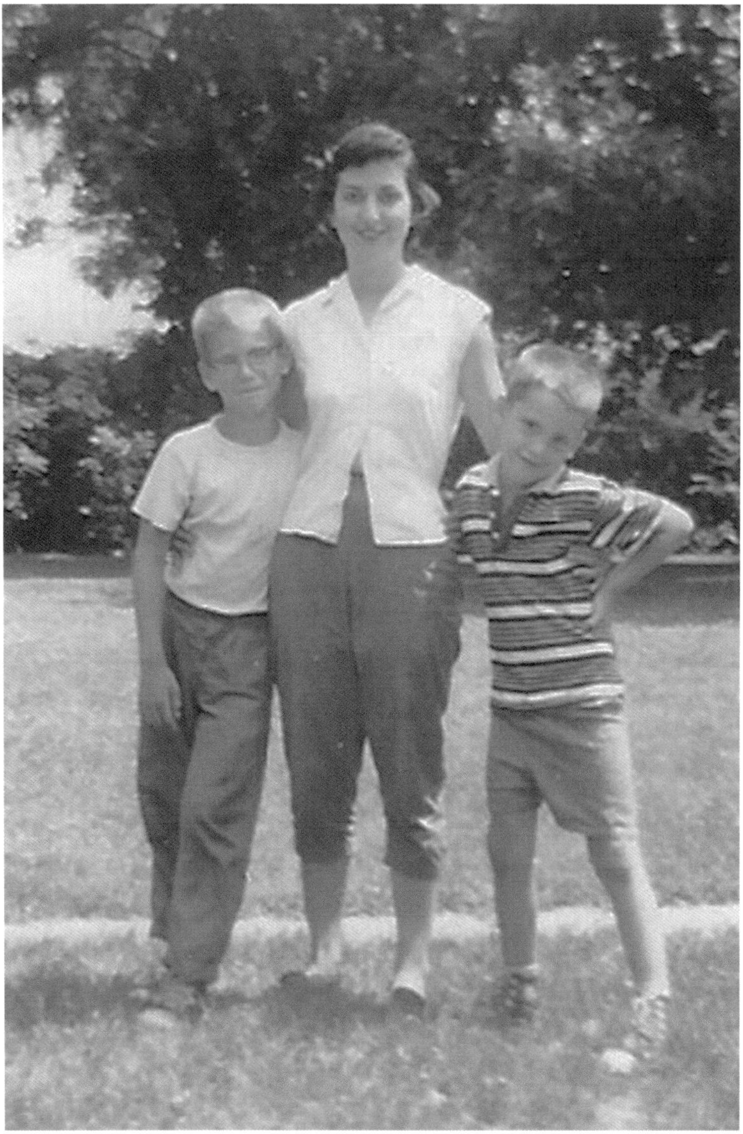

Dad

Marty Gabriel

My dad is having cancer surgery on Thursday and I'm anxious about it. He'll lose a kidney, a ureter, and some of his bladder, yet he approaches the operation stoically. He's an experienced patient and a good one. He almost lost an eye once when a retina nearly became detached. The doctor pulled the damaged eye out of its socket and put a buckle around it as my dad calmly watched with his good eye. He's also appreciative of my mother's aftercare, occasionally noting, "Without her I'd be dead."

Dad celebrated Easter very pleasantly with immediate and extended family members this past Sunday, and I can joyfully report he's mellowed quite a bit in his twilight years; things are better now that my brother and I have families of our own. Of course, there's still the occasional rant against Obama or "the liberals," or the odd outburst directed toward his oldest son and namesake for some egregious behavior, such as using too much A-1 sauce.

"I'm going to charge you for that like they were going to do at that Greek restaurant," he barked at me not very long ago when I was the only houseguest. Though I offered to pay immediately, this only seemed to infuriate him more.

"Quit being an asshole. That's a total insult to your mother's cooking, a total insult," he screamed.

"But, Dad, I haven't even opened the bottle yet, and I was only going to put a little on the veggies."

When a truce was quickly and silently established and civil conversation resumed ten minutes later, I was relieved the sudden storm had quickly passed.

Dad has always been moody and volatile at home, quick to harshly reprimand family members yet disinclined to own up to any of his own misbehavior. But he's also been a very responsible and reliable provider, one whose family is very important to him. When I was a youngster, my mother provided me with an explanation for this incongruity. She might have done this after I'd asked if I'd been adopted, thinking it might explain some mistreatment I'd suffered.

"Your dad had a very rough childhood, Butch," she said. "His dad used to drink too much, especially during the Depression when he was out of work. Your grandma told me how they'd have to pick him out of the bushes in front of their house after he'd pass out there on his way home from the tavern. But she said that was better than when he'd make it home because he was mean when he was drunk and he'd beat them if he made it home. When she came home from her job scrubbing floors one day after your grandfather had been looking after the kids, she found your dad curled up and shaking like a leaf in a corner of his crib like he'd been traumatized.

"She took the kids and ran away to California for a while, but eventually she missed your grandfather and came back. She had your dad and your Uncle Joe baptized in secret because your grandfather hated the church and wouldn't have allowed it. He'd been an altar boy and apparently something had happened to him or he'd seen something that changed him. When your dad was older, he had to be the one to stop your grandfather from beating Joe and Grandma."

My mom's voice cracked a bit as she continued, "Even now your dad will have nightmares that wake me up. I'll hear him whimpering and crying, saying, 'Don't hit me, don't hit me.' So there are reasons he is the way he is."

This made a great deal of sense to me and since then I've thought of my dad as being understandably flawed and also rather heroic in some very important ways. He certainly was a high achiever. He worked three jobs when my brother and I were young, coached us in Little League, and, along with my mom, paid the tuition that allowed my brother and me to attend expensive private colleges.

Professionally, he earned a reputation as a tough and innovative inner-city school administrator. As a school principal on the west side of Chicago, he courageously and practically forged a productive alliance with the Black Panthers, meeting with them to diffuse tension during turbulent times and instituting sickle cell anemia testing with their help in response to the needs of the community he served. He also became an outspoken advocate for the rights of physically disabled students. Parents, fellow administrators, and even gang leaders greatly respected his firmness, fairness, and ability to create safe, productive school environments in depressed neighborhoods. His effectiveness resulted in his receiving a series of difficult school assignments and his eventual promotion to an important job in the school system's central office. Years later when I worked in the same system as a school social worker on a citywide diagnostic team, I was proud to be known as "Marty Gabriel's son."

I've read that it takes at least a couple of generations to extinguish alcoholic family patterns, and my dad took pride in the fact that we never saw him drunk. He was doing a lot better than his father did as far as I could see, and as a youngster I decided it was important for me to continue this trend. I wouldn't eat rum cookies in high school and I didn't drink beer until my junior year of college. In my twenties, as a member of the Anheuser Busch Beercats, a semipro football team that competed nationally, I exposed myself to a great deal of ridicule and scorn by opting to drink grapefruit juice at the taverns where the team hung out.

My dad never talked much about his father. When asked about him, he'd usually just say he was a great father, except for one time when I was a middle-aged adult. I was in the back seat of the car with my wife-to-be when my dad unexpectedly let his emotional guard down after years and years of stonewalling.

"Yeah, I had a rotten father," he admitted softly and somewhat tearfully.

But just as he started to elaborate, my mother interrupted and minimized what he'd said. Dad's usual guardedness immediately resurfaced and the moment was lost. My mother's reaction frustrated me immensely, but I suppose she had her reasons for preserving the status quo. Change can be scary and it's not unusual for members of dysfunctional family systems to have feelings of security or control they resist giving up in favor of something healthier, but perhaps she just wanted to spare him the painful memories elaboration would certainly evoke.

Recently while cleaning out a closet I found an old box of letters I'd received in college. Many were from my dad and they routinely contained very endearing sentiments my dad would have been extremely unlikely to express face to face. They were also written in a more formal tone than my father would have used in person. I remembered receiving the letters, but they surprised me nonetheless.

In the midst of mundane news about immediate and extended family members were excerpts to be savored, such as the following.

> It was great talking to you the other day. I really miss you. It seems that we often have some heated discussions but quite often when I have had an opportunity to digest what you've said I find that even if I don't agree with your conclusions they do have merit and give me possible data to modify my position. I miss the youthful insight that you display in many areas.

One letter in particular caught my attention. It was most unusual in that it also included an apology. The letter was heartfelt and four pages long. It begins,

> Dear Son,
>
> I am writing this letter on the night of the day you left. I must write my thoughts down right away or I'll forget to tell you them.
>
> First off I apologize for acting so irrational Monday night. After I have some time to reflect on my actions I realize that they are quite juvenile and that my emotions get control over me. I want you to know that I love you very deeply and it is because of this that I overreact to some seemingly minor incident.

The letter concludes:
> I need your love and the rest of the family's. I may seem hard but I'm very emotional. I think that's why I blow up so fast.
>
> This is perhaps the first time I've expressed myself like this. I hope it doesn't sound too trite.
>
> I think very highly of you and have the utmost confidence in your ability to succeed. It may seem that I doubt you at times but I really don't.
>
> I'll close for now—You've been gone only 10 hours but already my heart is heavy and it seems that I always send you off with one of my outrages.
>
> Love,
> Dad

Sadly, while I had appreciated the sincere tone of this letter, the apology, and the admission of vulnerability when I'd received it, I had consciously dismissed it to a large extent as being another misleading instance of a letter-writing persona I felt my dad adopted to compensate for his verbal abusiveness without really determining to change his behavior. The very encouraging and upbeat letters I'd received previously had been followed by his much different, disparaging, and frequently hostile attitude when we were actually reunited for any length of time.

But this was another missed opportunity to move things along, to help heal the wounded. If I'd been more mature and wise, perhaps I would have written back the following:

> Dear Dad,
>
> I think you're very brave to apologize and acknowledge your vulnerabilities and needs. Your willingness to do these things makes you stronger, more admirable, and more loveable in my eyes.
>
> I'm also very emotional and vulnerable and although I may seem stubborn or even rebellious at times, I very much need

and appreciate your love, too.

I know you love me and I believe the remorse you expressed is genuine. I think you were deeply hurt a long time ago by your own father and I think this has a lot to do with why you sometimes feel compelled to treat me so badly and contrary to your better nature.

The heartfelt sentiments you expressed are far from trite.

Thanks for opening up and showing the gentle, considerate, and reflective side of your personality in a way I've never seen before.

To see that side of you more often will fill my heart with joy!
Your loving son,
Butch

Marty Gabriel

My parents grew up in Chicago during the Great Depression, the children of immigrants from Czechoslovakia and Greece. They fell in love at Chicago Teachers College, where both were majoring in physical education, and they started a family soon after graduation. I am grateful for my Bohemian and Spartan roots and very appreciative of my parents' grit, generosity, and many accomplishments.

Like my parents, I have a great love of sports and an inclination toward public service. After majoring in philosophy and graduating from Dartmouth College, where I played football and baseball, I taught and coached for several years before deciding to obtain a Master of Social Work degree.

However, competing in games has always been my primary avocation. Current pastimes include tennis, pool, ping pong, softball, bowling, and golf. As a Scrabble player I hold a record for most official games with a score of 700 or more points, and I have represented the United States at recent World Scrabble Championships in India, Malaysia, Poland, and the Czech Republic. Charitable endeavors include directing large Scrabble for Literacy events in Chicago and Danville and also directing the Charleston Scrabble Club (charlestonscrabbleclub.net). My muse/wife, Daiva Markelis, plays also, and we have been featured in the documentary *Scrabylon* and on *Central Illinois A to Z*. In 2007, I retired from my job as a Chicago school social worker, but I've lived happily in Charleston, Illinois, since 2005.

Harryetta

Jane Cavins Gilbert

Harryetta's persona was shaded with mystery before I ever met her. Her family moved to town and left her behind with her grandmother. I met her parents and Johnny and Nancy, her little brother and sister, and they all seemed normal enough. What was wrong with her? How bad would I have to be before my parents moved and left me behind?

We were both fourteen, ready to start high school when she finally appeared. At that age I wasn't eager to deal with strangers, and it wasn't in my nature to make the first move. But my father wanted me to "be nice to her," so on a Sunday afternoon I walked three blocks to her house and then we walked together up to the Will Rogers Theater to see a matinee. The movie that day was the western *Duel in the Sun*, and in it a very young and incredibly handsome Gregory Peck played the role of the villain. I had seen Gregory Peck in another movie and was already madly in love with him as only a fourteen-year-old can be with her first movie-star crush.

Walking home after that movie, Harryetta and I gushed together about Gregory Peck and went on to discover a shared fondness for romantic fantasies and for books and movies in general. My own sister was five years younger than I, and at that stage of our lives we had nothing in common. Harryetta's sister issues were even more complicated, I was to learn much later. That Sunday afternoon we each found a new sister and began a friendship that sustained us both through those four always-difficult years of high school.

We were in many classes together. We went to movies and basketball games together. We joined the same activities, except for biology club and choir. Harryetta did not sing; I had no interest in bugs. We read the same books and compared notes. We both idolized our French teacher and adored our handsome, young, and single history teacher. We even stalked him to a limited degree. On warm nights we would go for long walks around town, talking of school and books and boys and love and future plans. We always managed to walk past the house where we knew he lived, sometimes circling the block a time or two, and if there was a light on in the room we imagined was his, that made it even more exciting.

Our school was small, and everyone, both teachers and students, knew that if Harryetta was around, Jane was not far away and vice versa. After school we worked on both the yearbook and the newspaper. She preferred the former, I the latter, and as seniors we each became the editor of our preferred publication, but generally our efforts were mutual. Once we decided to write a serialized story for the newspaper to run in an unspecified number of consecutive editions. It was a hurried, unpolished effort, but it contained all of our favorite story elements: a handsome hero, a dastardly villain, a far-off mystical land, and, of course, unrequited love. After three episodes we got bored with it and killed off all the characters in one giant catastrophe. Miss Johnson, who sponsored the newspaper, published it anyway. I wonder now how we ever had the nerve to show our faces around the school after that, but at the time we thought we could do no wrong.

We both went out for the speech team, I in poetry reading, Harryetta in dramatic interpretation. Our classroom grades were about the same, but there was no question that when it came to talent, Harryetta was miles ahead of me. She was an actress. Give her a chance to be someone other than herself, and it was as if she stepped into a new skin. Even without training she knew how to speak and how to move. She always got the lead role in any school play, and audiences were always impressed. I don't think I was jealous of her talent because that wasn't something I aspired to, though I might have been a little jealous of the attention it brought her. Mainly I was jealous of her certainty about what she wanted to do with her life. She was going to go to New York and be an actress on the stage. She believed it wholeheartedly and so did I. I didn't know where life was going to take me, but I was pretty sure it would be nowhere near that glamorous.

And she was glamorous already. We were about the same height, both fairly slim with brown hair. But my hair was straight, I wore glasses and had normal adolescent skin blemishes. Harryetta's hair was softly curly, she didn't need glasses and had perfect creamy skin with just a hint of pink on her beautiful high cheekbones. Her face was a little too round and her nose had a bump in it that she didn't like; she wasn't conventionally beautiful, but she always looked great. She was what my mother would have called "well put together"; she just knew how to wear clothes. We went to school in the same kind of sweaters and skirts and bobby sox, but I looked like the girl next door before breakfast while she looked like someone out of the pages of *Seventeen* magazine. For our senior prom I wore a frilly blue and white number that my mother deemed "suitable." Harryetta came in wine velveteen. She looked terrific!

As close as we were, I knew surprisingly little about her family life. She was essentially a very private person. Her father was a tall man with a kind face, a gentle manner, and a twinkle in his eye. Dr. P. was a zoology professor, and we would occasionally find a dead ani-

PORTHOLE 1952

mal in their refrigerator, a squirrel or something like that. He always called me Margaret. The first few times I corrected him, explaining that Margaret was someone else—I was Jane. It made no difference; he still called me Margaret. Harryetta's mother was a beautiful redhead with those same high cheekbones and same sense of style. She taught English at Charleston High School for many years. Harryetta's parents and mine were fairly close friends, but my father disapproved, in private, of the fact that Mrs. P. worked outside her home "just because she wanted a nicer house and furniture than her friends." My own disapproval of her, which I could not have verbalized at the time, came from the fact that I sensed a coolness between her and Harryetta that both puzzled and worried me. It was clear to me that Mrs. P. preferred Johnny and Nancy over her older daughter.

After high school we went our separate ways. Harryetta stayed at home and attended Eastern Illinois, majoring in speech and theater. I went away to college and came home for summer vacations, but already our lives and interests had begun to diverge. The first summer I got a part-time job, worked in the evenings and spent my days at the swimming pool. Harryetta had a factory job and had to get up early in the morning. We went on a few double dates, but I could tell the close connection was broken. I would have written letters, but Harryetta was not a writer. Long-distance phone calls were expensive and at least in my family not to be used for visiting, only important business.

After college I married and had children. Harryetta went to New York and studied at the American Academy of Dramatic Arts for a while. She played some summer stock and got some bit parts in the city, but her acting career never flourished. She had talent, but I suspect she wasn't pushy enough and probably not "compliant" enough.

For many years the only word I had of her came through my parents. She would stop by to visit them when she came back to town to see her family, and then I would get a report. I learned that she eventually married a journalist and also that she became a teacher at the American Academy.

I always wondered what it would be like if we were ever to get together again, and I got to find out one summer when I was home for a visit and she was in town at the same time. I called her and we met at a restaurant for a glass of iced tea. As we described our lives to each other, it was apparent that we might as well have been living on different planets. I lived in a house in the suburbs, drove a Chevrolet, taught high-school students, and worried about the problems of 20-something offspring. She was childless, lived with her husband in an apartment in Manhattan, rode a cab to her teaching post at the American Academy, and went to cocktail parties with minor celebrities. The only thing we had in common was our aging and increasingly frail parents. She still looked terrific.

By the time I retired and moved back to Charleston, Harryetta's father had died and her mother had moved away to live with Nancy. Then one day I read her mother's obituary in the Charleston paper. "Preceded in death by...and one daughter, Harryetta." I was stunned. How could I not have known? I tracked Nancy down, called her and heard the whole story. It had happened several years before; she must have been still in her 50s. She was getting out of a taxi on her way to work when a bicycle messenger hit her and she fell, striking her head against a curb. She lay in a coma for several days and then died. Nancy sent me an article from *The New York Times* describing the tribute paid to her by the American Academy of Dramatic Arts. They called her "one of our finest, most respected and beloved teachers."

I learned from my mother sometime in my adult years that Harryetta's own mother had died, leaving her husband with three small children, and he had then married his wife's sister. Johnny and Nancy bonded with their stepmother/aunt, but Harryetta did not. This explained both the family resemblance and the coolness. It also told me how little I really knew her.

Leaving

Jane Cavins Gilbert

"I'm going and I'm never coming back," he said angrily, his hand on the doorknob.

The woman across the room started toward him, then stopped. "I'm going to miss you," she said softly.

He slammed the door behind him and stomped down the steps. Then he got on his tricycle and peddled away.

Thanksgiving
in Fifty-Five Words

Jane Cavins Gilbert

I cleaned. I planned. I shopped. I baked. They arrived. We hugged. We cooked and ate. We made a mess and cleaned it up. We watched football and worked a jigsaw puzzle. We lit a fire in the grate. We talked and laughed and remembered. It was all wonderful. We hugged. They left. I slept.

Renaissance

Jane Cavins Gilbert

I HARDLY DATED AT ALL when I was in high school. Not that I wouldn't have liked to, but I was rather shy and pretty studious and had no idea how to talk to boys, who hardly noticed me anyway. My mother tried to reassure me by saying that when I got to college, I would meet men who were more mature and who would find me interesting and attractive, but for the most part, she was wrong. I did have a few dates, but there was never any spark; they mostly seemed like losers to me. The desirable ones still seemed to prefer girls who knew how to dress and talk and flirt.

In a senior English class I sat down at my desk the very first day, and Richard was sitting just across the aisle next to me. It was a small-enough college that an upperclassman knew everyone at least by sight, and this was someone I had never seen before. He was not the movie-star-handsome man of my dreams, but he was good-looking in a boy-next-door sort of way with freckles and curly hair and a winning smile, and when he talked to me, he made me feel like the most important person in the world. We actually had a casual conversation. I was relaxed and not tongue-tied; he talked to me as if I was a real person. After class we walked together across campus to the union. And not too many days later, he asked me out on a date.

He had been a student at the college and should have graduated three years earlier, but he had dropped out of school, been drafted, and gone to Korea. With his military service out of the way and a new mature attitude toward school, he had come back to finish his education under the GI Bill. Our one date led to others, and neither of us dated anyone else after that. I had met the mature man who found me interesting and attractive, and what is more attractive in a man than that? Naturally I married him.

He came from a blue-collar family, I from an academic one. He was only three years older than I, but he had been in the army, had seen something of the world, and had fended for himself emotionally and sometimes physically for much of his life. I'd had a very sheltered upbringing, had never really been out of the nest, and knew very little about men and nothing at all about the male psyche.

But the biggest difference of all between us was in what we expected of marriage and family life. His model was of an alcoholic father and a strong mother who kept the family together but survived by detaching herself emotionally. Mine was of a father whose number-one priority was his family and a mother, also strong, who played the submissive role and managed things behind the scenes. None of these differences were ever spoken of or even realized until far too late.

Our first year and a half of marriage was essentially a long honeymoon in New York City. We found a tiny inexpensive apartment in Manhattan. He got a job as a reporter for a construction news publication. I got a low-level job at the United Nations through a friend of my parents. Neither of us made much money, but we had enough to live on and a little left over to go to the theater every week, sometimes twice a week. We learned all the tricks for getting cheap tickets, and every once in a while we would splurge. I think we saw every show on Broadway that season and most of off-Broadway as well. We saw a very young Jason Robards Jr. in *Long Day's Journey into Night*; we saw Rosalind Russell in *Mame*, and we saw Rex Harrison and Julie Andrews in *My Fair Lady*, among many others. We went to all the museums and historical sites and explored the city with any free time we had. For me, that year and a half was more of an education than four years of college.

After that came graduate school at the University of Iowa. Carolyn was born that year. Richard was working on a master's degree in theater and loving every minute of it. My own decision to work on a master's in Spanish was simply a reaction to being bored and lonely, a glimpse of how my life was going to be from now on.

Next came a year in Maryville, Missouri, and the arrival of our daughter Diane, two more years of graduate school, then off to a teaching job in Minot, North Dakota, and the birth of Daniel. I liked a lot of things about Minot. It offered a wealth of amenities for a town of its size, I felt right at home in the college atmosphere, and I had friendly neighbors, though none my own age. But the winters were long and hard, and I was alone with three small children much of the time. I disliked cooking and housekeeping and felt frustrated that I wasn't much good at either. I started feeling as if I wasn't much good at anything.

The marriage limped along for several more years. I longed for the kind of quiet, ordinary family life my parents had had; Dick relished his work, with irregular hours and unconventional people and lots of attention focused on him. I felt he was neglecting his family; he felt I was hampering his career. I thought he was selfish; he thought I was boring. We were both right. We tried marriage counseling and even survived two separations and reconciliations. But we had grown in different directions, and there was no place we could find to meet in the middle.

The divorce after eighteen years of marriage could hardly be called friendly, but it was probably less rancorous than most. Both of us finally realized that not only were we not making each other happy, we probably never would; our expectations and goals were simply too different. In the next five years, I met and married Steve, a kind and comfortable man with a background similar to mine. And Dick found Kate, someone from his world who was wise and tolerant and made him happy.

That should be the end of Richard's role in my life, but it's not. Just a few years into our new marriages, our son Dan, then going on 20, was hospitalized and diagnosed with severe depression. Various medical plans had to be discussed, decisions had to be made, and financial matters also had to be considered. Dick and Kate came to our house where Steve and I sat down with them to talk. It was awkward at first, but our main concern was with someone other than ourselves and we soon discovered that we could work together rationally, even cordially, and come up with a plan.

That traumatic event in all our lives, terrible as it was, led to some surprising and positive results. Dan got the treatment he needed and has turned out rather well. And that first awkward conversation led to others and eventually to a smooth and even friendly working relationship between our two families that got us through birthdays, weddings, and the arrival of the grandchildren. Everybody benefited. Our children have given us lots of credit for making their lives easier. They all have friends with divorced parents who can't be in the same room with each other without making things unpleasant for everyone around them. Ours always knew that if they wanted to invite the four of us to a birthday party, we'd come and behave ourselves.

The years passed. Steve and I retired, did a lot of traveling, and enjoyed long vacations at our lake cabin in Minnesota. Dick and Kate acquired a large vacation home on Cape Hatteras in North Carolina and would invite the children and grandchildren to come and stay. I enjoyed hearing their stories about days at the beach, but I was never

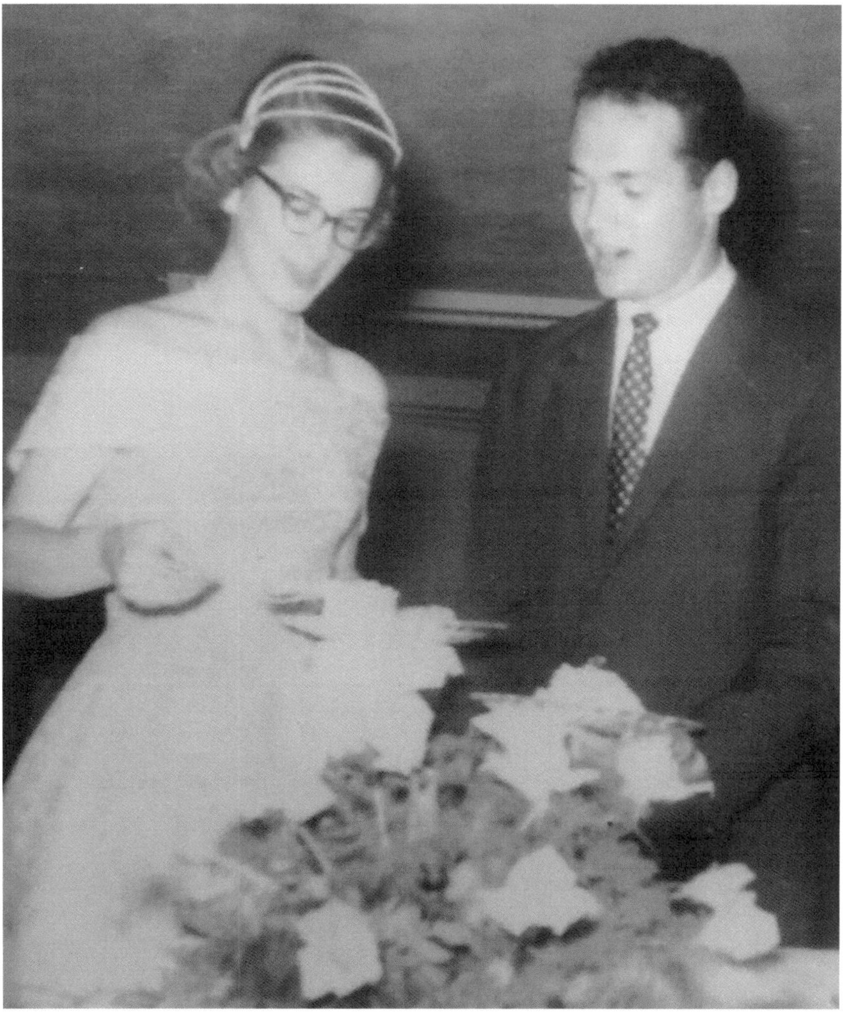

jealous of their time with their father. Holidays were not a problem; nobody got neglected. We were all comfortable with each other.

But Steve's health began to fail, and he died just short of our twenty-fifth anniversary. I grieved, but I gradually adjusted to my new life. Late in November that year, I got a call from Dan, a rare occurrence in itself, but this one astounded me. After a few amenities, he got to the point:

"What will you be doing for Christmas this year?" he asked.

Dan is not noted for long-range planning, and he generally leaves concern for his mother's welfare up to his sisters. It took me a few moments to take in and process the question.

"I don't know," I told him, "but I'm sure something will turn up."

"Well," he said, "you should come up here and spend Christmas with us." More red flags! Dan's wife is Jewish; there is no Christmas tree or Christmas dinner at their house. "Of course that means you'd have to spend Christmas Day at Dick and Kate's."

"And what would Kate think about that?" I asked. After all, cordiality is one thing, but inviting the ex-wife for Christmas is something else entirely.

"It was her idea," was the answer.

So I went. I was welcomed warmly and had a beautiful Christmas with my son and his wife, my grandchildren, and my ex-husband and his wife. It was a beginning.

Sometime in the spring of the following year I got a phone call from Dan's wife, Jill. No red flags there; she is a sweetheart and does call me occasionally. But this time she had me speechless:

"We think you should come to Hatteras in August with the family this year," she said.

Again I asked, "But what would Kate think about that?"

And I got the same answer; "It was her idea."

It's a two-day drive from Charleston, Illinois, to Hatteras, North Carolina. I have made that trip every summer for the past nine years.

It is the highlight of my year. I get to see my children and grandchildren and whatever other assorted relatives happen to be there. I sit on the beach or splash in the surf, read a good book or two, play cards, work on a jigsaw puzzle. I buy a few groceries, prepare a couple of meals, and get to eat other people's cooking the rest of the time. I can't wait for August next year.

And I have spent the same number of Christmases at Dick's and Kate's home. They now come to my house for Thanksgiving. Our children love it; they don't have to go two places for the holiday. We have developed our own habits and customs. Kate and I have become almost good friends. She is a lovely person — small in stature but a giant in understanding and good will. She has been a kind and loving stepmother and grandmother to my children and grandchildren. I still can't quite figure out why she is willing to put up with me; I'm not sure I would be equally gracious if our situations were reversed. But I am sure that she is the person who has made all this possible. It is a blessing for which I am thankful every day.

When I look at Richard these days, I find it hard to remember that I was once married to him. He is someone else's husband now and I am very glad of it. He still likes to be the center of attention, but his agenda is no longer the only one that counts. He has matured some over the years, as I have as well. And there are moments when I recall why I was so happy to marry him fifty-five years ago. He is still charming and funny and intelligent, and when he talks to you, he makes you feel like the most important person in the world. A better friend than husband perhaps, but a very good friend indeed.

Alone

Jane Cavins Gilbert

GRETA GARBO, THE STUNNINGLY beautiful movie star who has been called one of the five greatest film actresses of all time, retired at age thirty-five at the height of her success because she just wanted to be left alone. She is an extreme example of a person with the solitude gene. People who don't have this gene can't understand why anyone would choose to be alone when social contact is available. People who have it find occasional solitude is as necessary as food and sleep; when we are deprived of it, we are not living our most fulfilling lives.

I have the solitude gene. I usually don't put it into those words. My words are more likely to be, "If I don't get away from these people pretty soon, I'm going to go bonkers!" "These people" could very well be the ones I love the most; I would just love them a little more if I could see a little less of them.

I was well into my adult years before I realized this about myself, although looking back I can see the early signs. I was an only child for five years until my little sister came along, and perhaps that conditioning was enough to make me accept being alone as a natural state. I cannot remember any time in my life when I felt that "alone" was a bad or a frightening thing.

As a child I always looked forward to school and to being with my friends. In college I lived in dormitories for four years, so being alone was never an option, though I do remember finding the solitude of a library carrel a welcome retreat. Then I got married and raised three children and taught high-school students, and for many years there was hardly ever a time when I was alone, and if I was, I was too tired to appreciate it.

Then one year I was asked to visit another high school for three days as part of an evaluation team. For two nights I had a hotel room all to myself. It made me so happy I didn't want to go to sleep and waste it. I just wanted to sit there and read or watch TV, knowing the phone wouldn't ring and no one would appear at my door saying, "Mom, can you find my blue sweater?" That's when I first consciously realized I needed some solitude in my life.

The high school where I taught allowed us a full class period—fifty minutes—for lunch. I could generally eat mine in twenty or twenty-five. Afterward I would go to the teachers' lounge, but now instead of sitting down to socialize as I formerly did, I would find the daily newspaper scattered around in sections after twenty or so people had read it, grab the crossword puzzle and take it to my classroom where I would shut the door and work the puzzle in complete silence. I came to look forward to that little oasis of solitude, and I know it helped me get through those afternoon classes that always seemed to require more energy than the morning ones.

I thought that after I retired, it would be easier for me to find a little "alone time" time each day, but the opposite proved to be true. My husband could not even conceive of the solitude gene. He wanted as much company as possible. He had been retired for several years and was the world's best househusband. But now that I no longer had to go to work, he imagined we were going to be together all day, every day. And that was just fine with him. He was a wonderful husband and I loved him, but not THAT much.

If I tried to escape into a book, he felt free to interrupt me. Steve liked to read if he had nothing better to do, but he considered it an activity to fill the time until something more social came along. I tried to explain to him that when I was reading I was "busy," but he couldn't really process that information. So just as I'd get to the most exciting page, I would hear, "Get your coat, we're going to the hardware store," or "We're going out to lunch," or "We're going to run over to the mall," and I would put in the bookmark and go. Maybe I should have just said no, but Steve was not easy to say no to, and you pick your battles. Besides, I found a better solution.

After I had a mild heart attack at age fifty-nine, my doctor recommended daily exercise, which I knew I should have been doing anyway but hadn't done very diligently. Now highly motivated, I began going for walks and discovered that while I didn't particularly relish the physical exercise, I loved the mental refreshment it gave me. I could be alone for an hour with no excuses. For the last twenty years I have walked by myself nearly every day. If some well-meaning soul offers to "keep me company," I politely decline. This is my thinking time, I tell them, and I just need to do it alone—I don't want to have to use my breath for talking; I want to use it to keep up the best pace I can. I also have work to do. I solve my problems, or some of them; I think up clever remarks I could have made to people I met yesterday; I write letters to friends or stories about my life. Sometimes I even come home and put them down on paper. Sometimes I pray, and sometimes I just look at the trees and squirrels and sidewalks and the bizarre clothing of the students I see. It is the best part of my day.

I no longer need the excuse of walking to find solitude. I am at the alone stage of my life; I have been a widow for the past ten years. After an initial period of grief and adjustment, I discovered that living alone agrees with me. In my seventy years, I had never lived alone before. I had gone from my parents' home to college, then immediately into marriage, to divorced with teenagers, and then to another marriage. I knew how to pay bills, call the plumber, and get the car serviced, but I had never before eaten supper alone on a regular basis or gotten into and out of bed with the rest of the house completely quiet. And I liked it.

As I watch more and more of my female friends enter this world of living alone, I find it interesting to see which ones take to it as I did. Some never do, but for others it seems like the beginning of a whole new life, and I don't think this is any reflection of who misses her husband the most. I'm pretty certain that women are better at living alone than men are, though I can't say why. My own reasons go something like this: I can now come and go exactly as I please; I can eat or not eat whatever I want whenever I want; I can spend money as I choose without having to consult anyone; and I have complete control of the remote. It's not a bad way to live.

I am now so accustomed to my aloneness that I miss it sorely when it is lacking. When I am with a group of people for an extended period, such as having guests at my home or visiting at someone else's house or going on vacation with family, I find myself looking for excuses to get away by myself. "I'll be glad to run to the grocery store and get those things you need. No, you don't need to come with me. I can manage." Or I simply find a lounge chair and a book and disappear for an hour. I once took a trip with a tour group where our schedule was so tightly managed that there was no time to get away from the group during the day. I was so tired at the end of the day that I could hardly function after eight o'clock. It wasn't physical tiredness but mental exhaustion from too many people around me for too long.

I suspect that the solitude gene is a requisite for any kind of creative endeavor. Most writers, artists, and inventors seem to flourish best when given a lot of space. And people who go into solitary professions must have the gene to some degree leading them in that direction. My son-in-law chose a second career as a watchmaker and repairer. He sits for hours by himself in a small room at a workbench looking through a loupe and manipulating tiny bits of things that look to me like the crumbs I sweep up off my kitchen floor. It suits him just fine.

I'm not sure that much solitude would suit me. When I was teaching, I valued my alone time with the crossword puzzle, but then I was happy to see students walking through my classroom door again. Today I have arranged my life so that while many of my evenings are spent alone, almost every day I have some activity that gets me out of the house and into the company of other people, even if it's just a trip to the dentist or the grocery store. And most days it's more than that. I visit friends or go to lunch with them, I play bridge, I go to meetings (lots of meetings!), I deliver meals to shut-ins, I greet visitors at Lincoln Log Cabin, I go to church and handbell practice and the library, and everywhere I go, I interact with people and enjoy their company. I don't want to be a hermit. But then I go home and eat my supper alone, turn on the TV for a while, usually turn it off again and pick up a book or sit down at the computer and write. I enjoy the silence around me.

And I am not lonely.

Jane Cavins Gilbert

I GREW UP in a family of letter writers and became one myself when I went to camp at age thirteen, so in a sense I've been writing about myself most of my life. For more than fifty years I wrote regular letters to my parents telling them what I was doing. In clearing out their house, I found all the letters I had written home from college. Much of the content is embarrassingly juvenile, but in reading them I can see that I was practicing for what I'm doing today.

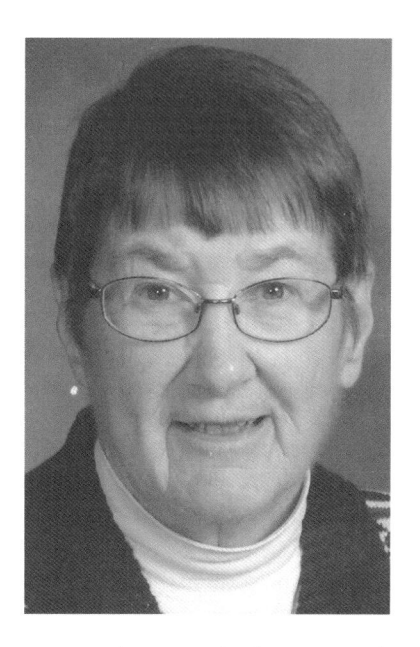

About five years ago I attended a meeting and sat by chance next to Janet Messenger, whom I knew hardly at all. As we made small talk, she told me about a memoir-writing group that had just gotten started, and I knew immediately that this was something I wanted to be part of. I had thought at times about trying to tell some of my stories, but I needed the motivation of a group to get started.

There are so many pleasures in being part of Past~Forward. I relish the satisfaction of putting into words some important and not-so-important events of my life and the joy of sharing them with others. I have discovered the heady intoxication of hearing laughter as I read aloud. Best of all I have made new friends and heard their own amazing stories.

Thank you, Past~Forward. This has been a life-changing experience for me.

San Francisco Penny

Gaye Harrison

So here I stand, Illinois flatlander, outside a big hotel in awe of San-by golly-Francisco, catching a cab up to the Castro to Andrea's apartment. I hop in, amped up with excitement, and drill my cabbie on everything I can about him and the city.

"Is beautiful city, am tenor in San Francisco choral. Been very happy here three year."

I find this thrilling, two degrees of separation from the Kremlin! I ask about the Exploratorium in Golden Gate Park since I have passes for a fabulous PBS cocktail party on Thursday evening and will invite Andrea to go.

"Is excellent. Will be most great for friend and you."

And here's my stop. Thank you, nice tip, up the steps, enter the apartment and am awash in new faces at the party held in my honor.

I start to tell my new friends all about the Exploratorium and make plans to meet Andrea there after my Thursday conference sessions. I go to grab the tickets out of my portfolio that is…somewhere. I'm not finding it. I'm panicked. My stomach is knotting up.

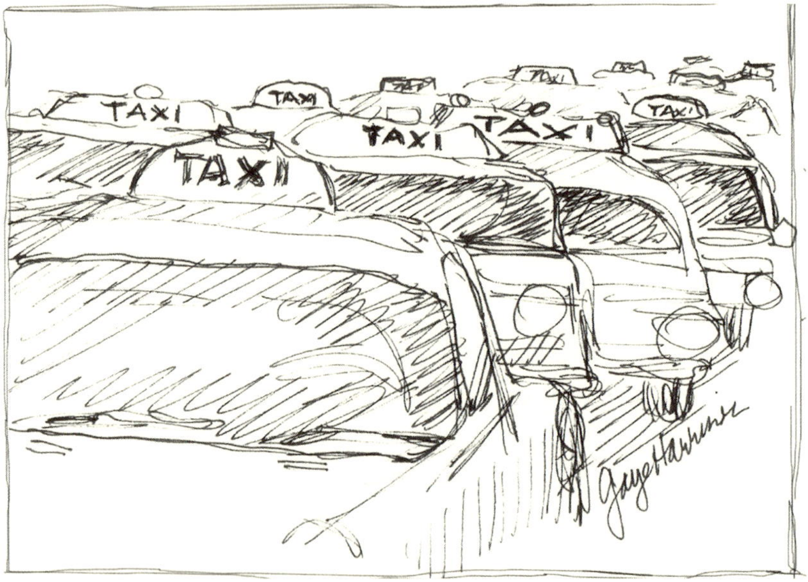

"Did you leave it in the taxi?" one partier asks. My heart sinks. Yes, that IS where I left it.

I have to get it back.

It has my schedule, my airplane ticket, Exploratorium tickets. Okay, let's see. "My taxi was yellow," I tell the partiers, intent on getting their help since they are natives. I hear a few titters, but think surely it has nothing to do with me. "And the driver was a Russian tenor." Larger laughs. "No, I don't know the name of the taxi company, but how hard would it be to find this particular taxi. What? HOW many taxi companies in San Francisco?" My heart sinks. I've never felt so hayseed, but I valiantly shrug it off and make some margaritas out of lemons. Chalk this one up to whatever.

I wake up the next morning with resolve to forget this bungle-brained mistake and call a new taxi to get back downtown for the conference. My new driver gets a full, forlorn recount of the lost portfolio debacle. I offer him a lone penny I spot on the floor, since it is technically his because it's in his vehicle. He declines and says I can have it. I try to explain the importance of luck and the penny, but who am I to lecture on that topic?

As we ride along, I feel stupid and embarrassed. And it doesn't help hearing my new driver reiterate the needle in a haystack and no chance in Hades concepts. Boy, is he having fun with this.

I ride the rest of the way with my head down until we're almost to the conference center. As we reach a red light, I glance out the window to my right, and there he is, my Russian taxi driver! Our eyes meet. I squeal to my new taxi driver "That's him, that's him!"

My Russian and I roll our windows down in synchronicity and he hands me my portfolio. "You left in taxi. Is yours, no?"

"Is mine, YES!" Dizzy from this miraculous transaction, laughing, feeling flushed, tearing up, I begin a crescendo of profuse thank-yous, but, too quickly, the light turns green and we're off.

Riding on with my first big smile since yesterday, I can feel the good karma settling around me. With reverence and a touch of awe, my new taxi driver says, "Ma'am, I'll take that penny."

Gaye Harrison

Gaye retired in 2011, and she continues to enjoy teaching fiddle and mandolin, and sharing Illinois old-time and Irish tunes with both her students and Motherlode audiences. Motherlode String Band (Gaye, Althea Pendergast, and Wendy Meyer) have been performing for more than two and a half decades. In 1977, Gaye moved to Charleston and became mandolin player for the Indian Creek Delta Boys, named State Band of Illinois in 1980 by the Illinois Legislature.

Gaye spent the early 1980s becoming a new mother to her daughter, Genevieve, and assisting her husband, Garry Harrison (Delta Boy fiddler), with collecting old-time tunes in downstate Illinois through a National Endowment for the Arts grant that funded field recording of traditional music, with selections archived in the Library of Congress. The Charleston Chamber of Commerce named Motherlode members as Citizens of the Year in 2010, citing their volunteer support of community organizations through music.

Art is also in Gaye's repertoire; she is past director of I Sing the Body Electric, a teen arts and health program of Sarah Bush Lincoln Health Center. Retirement provides her the opportunity to do graphic design and promotion for not-for-profit organizations in the area, including HOPE coalition against domestic violence. Gaye holds a BA in art education from Augustana College, Rock Island, Illinois, and an MA from the University of Illinois, Champaign.

The Most Amazing Lady
I Have Ever Known

❋

Dorothy Helland

My mother Millie was married at 19 and within nine years had five children: Dick, Marilyn, Carolyn, David, and me. As sometimes happens, the marriage was not on solid ground and dissolved before my parents' fifteenth anniversary. Everyone seemed to think Mother could not support her family. One time the church ladies came to our door with a turkey and fixings for Thanksgiving Dinner. Mother looked them in the eyes and said, "Take the food to a family that needs it. I can provide a Thanksgiving dinner for my children." Another time, her mother and sister-in-law came by the house and suggested she put her children in an orphanage. Needless to say, that did not go over so well either. My mother was a proud and very determined lady. She managed to buy the house we were living in for $600, a lot of money back then.

Sundays were a very special day for us, as Mother never worked on Sundays. After church we'd have a delicious dinner, then Mother would sit down at our upright piano and all five of us would sing along. I remember singing one of Nat King Cole's songs, "What'll

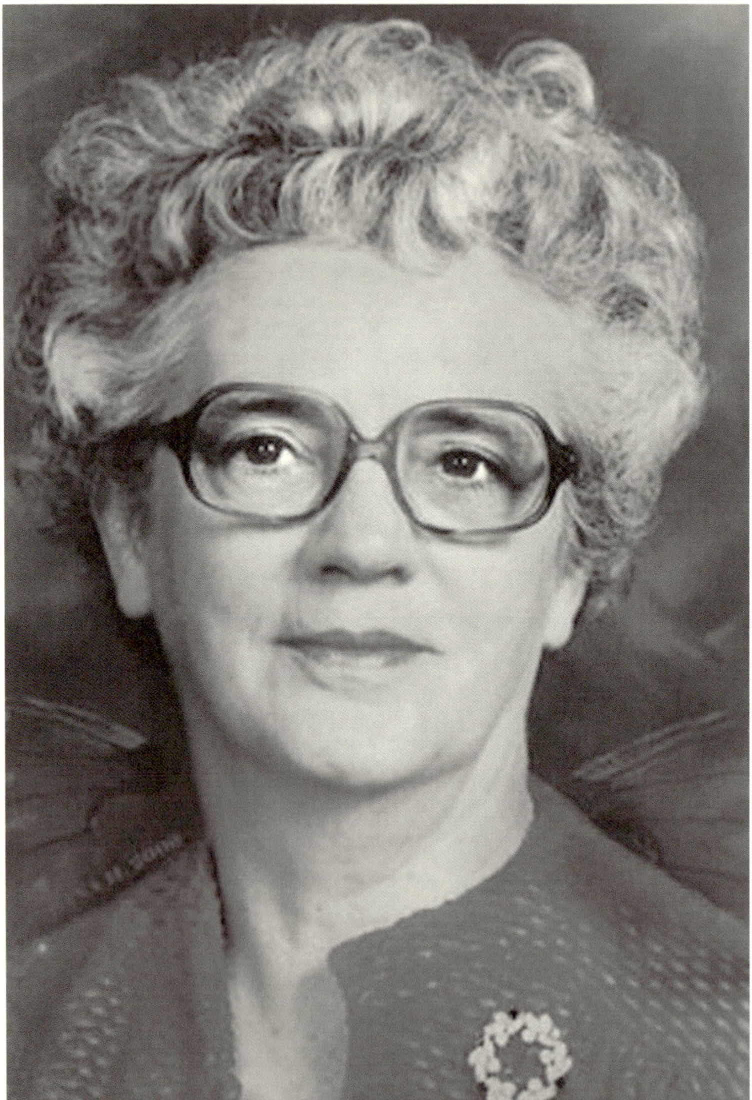

I Do." She loved Nat King Cole and even got to see him in person once — she was thrilled. Another memory regarding the upright piano: Mother hid our Christmas gifts behind it! I am positive she never knew we ALL peeked.

In the early years, she supported us by working as a waitress at the Kirwan, a high-class restaurant where they carried their trays high over their heads. The owners, Alex and Ada Mackres, made sure Mother worked the lunch hours and then came back for the supper hours — the best tip times. So she was there for us when the school bus came in the morning, then again when we came home from school. In the mornings, the bus driver would wait in front of our house while the five of us hugged and kissed our mother good-bye. After a while she had to tell us to stop this because we were holding up the school bus.

When I was 11, the Mackreses wanted to open a Marathon diner in Toledo, Ohio, and they wanted Mother to manage it for them. The first trips to Toledo were very exciting for Mother. She was walking in downtown Toledo, gaping at the many tall buildings. Alex, in his Greek accent, once said to Mother, "Millie, quit looking up. You are looking like a heek!" The Mackreses stayed in Lima, Ohio as my mother took on the responsibility of running the business for them. It was a huge success. My oldest brother, Dick, was in the Air Force by then, but our sisters carhopped, and my brother Dave and I "worked" for a nickel an hour and all the cheeseburgers, French fries, and milkshakes we could eat.

Three years later, Mother's father passed away. She could not bear the thought of her mother being alone, so she gave up running the diner and moved the three of us to Fort Wayne, Indiana. By then the twins were married and raising their families. My brother Dave and I were in high school. Mother went back to school while waitressing to support us, of course. When she learned what she felt she needed to work in an office, she started looking for a job. She was hired by St. Joseph Hospital as a clerk. She LOVED it. She worked herself up to Insurance Office Manager and could not have been happier.

At that time, there were nuns all over the place, working and assisting at the hospital. Mother had a special friend, Sister Pascales. The office ladies and the sisters would spend a day at the lake and have dinner together at their homes. Mother would have them all to her place for dinner and card games. She made a great Brandy Alexander for after dinner that the nuns really liked. I think in another life my mother would come back as a nun.

During Mother's retirement years she did travel, as her children lived in Kansas, Illinois, Ohio, and Pennsylvania, in addition to Indiana. She went to New York City with her daughters and saw Mary Tyler Moore on stage and also ate lunch at the famous Sardi's restaurant. As we were looking around at all the movie stars' pictures on the walls, we realized there was a famous person two tables away—Charles Nelson Reilly. We were thrilled, especially Mother. We did control ourselves and didn't ask for an autograph.

When Mother would fly out to Pennsylvania to see my family, we'd go to the Dutch restaurants and stores. The mushroom capital of the world was close by. There was so much to see, and she wanted to see it all—we probably would not have taken in all the great sights if not for her visits. She would always get a one-way ticket to visit us, and then I would drive her back home to Indiana. One year we decided to drive on to Kansas to visit with Dick's family—of course we went sightseeing on the way. I am so glad to have great memories from those days.

At dinner one night, I ordered a margarita. My mother was not drinking because of the medication she was taking. I apparently was licking my lips from the salt on the glass rim. The next thing I noticed was mother indicating to the waitress that she wanted what I was drinking. I started laughing and told her I was going to tell on her to her doctor.

I feel so honored to have had that great lady in my life. I will miss her forever.

Dorothy Helland

I was born in Lima, Ohio, the youngest of five children, including twin sisters and two brothers. Family has always been important to me, a concept instilled by my mother — my idol. A proud, determined woman, she led by example, demonstrating a strong work ethic, love, honesty and a delightful Irish sense of humor. She raised the five of us by waitressing, managing a restaurant, and later in life working as an office manager in a hospital.

My first job was waitressing (no surprise there), followed by working in a warehouse. I've had experience owning and operating two businesses with my husband, and later I moved on to become a supervisor of several departments at Consolidated Telephone Company before retirement when my husband and I hit the road in our RV.

I love writing and remembering stories about my husband Bill, my daughters, family, friends, and travels. I enjoy people and always try to look on the bright side of life.

The Salesman

Bill Heyduck

When I was in fifth grade, I decided I needed to find a better way to earn money so that I could pay my way into the Saturday movies. Digging around in alleys for pop bottles and newspapers was not only hard work, but it was also a very unreliable means of acquiring income. Movies were not my only goal for wanting to make some money. I also dreamed of owning a good baseball glove and ice skates that had shoes attached to them. Shoveling snow in the winter at fifteen cents a sidewalk and mowing lawns in the summer for twenty-five cents a lawn never amounted to more than the price of a movie ticket and a bag of popcorn.

My brother, sister, and I always went to the Saturday movies together so any money earned was shared when buying the movie tickets. My biggest disadvantage was that after knocking on a door and making my request to mow a lawn, the homeowner would take one look at my sixty-five pound frame and my big push mower and decline my offer. One day a woman accepted my offer of twenty-five cents to mow her lawn. She stood on her porch and watched me make every trip up and down her lawn as I mowed. When I was done, she made me mow it again going a different direction to make sure I didn't leave any little sprigs of grass. It didn't take me very long to realize I was never going to make enough to buy a ball glove with these meager earnings.

One fall day after school, I found my opportunity to join the commercial world through retail sales. Just outside the boundary of the schoolyard, I noticed a man standing behind a Ford panel truck, its back doors open and a group of boys gathered around him. I wandered over to see what was going on. As I approached, I heard him explaining how a boy could sell magazines. For each magazine sold, he could earn a certificate that could be redeemed for merchandise. The vendor had this merchandise displayed in the back of his truck. My eyes glazed over as I viewed all the wonderful things spread out before me. Ball gloves, hunting knives, bows and arrows, all the things I always dreamed of owning. The man said they could be mine with the sale of a few magazines. Before I knew what I was doing, I had a canvas bag with a broad canvas strap over my shoulder and nine magazines tucked inside it. I had three each of Saturday Evening Post, American Magazine, and Country Gentleman. I was on my way to earning some of those glittering prizes.

That night I told my parents about my new venture in capitalism. I didn't receive the enthusiastic response from them I had envisioned. Dad stated flatly that magazine sales could only start after my chores were completed. I only heard half of what he said. My head was filled with visions of all those glorious prizes displayed in the back of that panel truck.

The following day I rushed home from school, did my chores, grabbed my canvas bag of magazines, and headed out the door. I decided to start my new enterprise on my own street because I knew most of the people living there. I had a little speech worked out, and I repeated it in my head as I boldly walked up to the first door. A woman answered, but before I could say a word, she said she didn't know what I was selling, but she didn't need any and shut the door in my face with a solid thump. Undeterred, I rushed on to the next house and knocked. I heard people inside and even thought I saw someone look out from behind a curtain, but my knocking went unanswered.

Undiscouraged, I trudged on to the next house where a woman was sweeping her front porch. I approached her smiling and gave her my practiced sales pitch. She listened quietly until I finished, which raised my expectations, before telling me she subscribed to all the magazines she needed. Up and down the street I went knocking on doors and being sent away empty-handed. These were not the booming sales the magazine representative had led me to expect. Undeterred, I decided that maybe I needed to get out of my own neighborhood. Tomorrow, after school, I would go two or three blocks away from my street and try my luck.

The next day, I rushed home again, did a few chores, grabbed my bag of magazines, and took off with high hopes for improved sales. At the first house, no one answered so I rushed on to the next house and started up the walk. I had taken about three steps when I noticed a red ball of fur on the porch. In the middle of this ball of red fur were two piercing eyes looking straight at me. I froze in my tracks. I had to decide whether to go on up the walk or retreat. Before I could move either direction, the red ball of fur reared up on four legs and bared its white teeth. The red ball of fur had morphed into a fierce-looking Chow dog. I decided those people probably didn't read magazines anyway and retreated with slow trembling steps back to the street. I skipped the next two houses to put distance between me and the Chow. The second day ended just as the first one had, with no sales. I was beginning to get discouraged. Those fancy prizes were beginning to lose some of their luster.

Each night I went out with a little less enthusiasm and each night I trudged home with all the magazines I had started with. All I got at each door were excuses for not buying one of my magazines or people yelling at me for disturbing their rest or waking their baby. I was finding out that a door-to-door salesman had to develop a really thick skin.

I was ready to give it all up when I made my first sale. A man bought a magazine because he said he remembered trying to sell things when he was a kid and he remembered how tough it was. Then a woman two doors down from this man bought one because she felt sorry for me having to sell magazines to help support my family in these hard times. I didn't tell her I was selling magazines to win prizes; I just took her money, smiled, and tried to look sad.

At the end of the week, I reported my sales to the man with the panel truck and was surprised at how little I had sold compared to some of the other kids. The magazine representative said not to be discouraged, that it was always slow in the beginning. I turned in my money and all my unsold magazines and received the two certificates I was due. I was surprised to find out that the certificates for the prizes had different values according to your sales and I had received just two of the lesser ones.

Discouraged but determined, I picked up my nine new magazines, turned to go, and just happened to bump into a guy who had been one of the top sellers that week. Eager to find his secret of salesmanship, I questioned him on how he had done so well. He said he sold his magazines to the ladies of his mother's church group when they met at his house. The boy next to him volunteered that his father owned a grocery store and he sat in the store and sold them to his father's customers. Their stories gave me an idea on how to improve my sales.

My father was the superintendent at the Midwest Ice Cream Company and a lot of people worked for him at the ice cream plant. The next day after school, I headed for the ice cream plant with my new load of magazines. I didn't tell Dad, I just walked in to the plant and approached people with my sales pitch. I sold some magazines right away and thought I had struck the mother lode. I didn't realize that the buyers may have felt pressured because I was the boss's son. Dad saw me and asked what I was doing there. When he discovered my reason for being in the plant, he escorted me out and told me not to come back selling anything.

At the end of the third week, I realized I was not cut out to be a door-to-door salesman. I met the magazine representative at his Ford panel truck at the end of the week and turned in my unsold magazines and my magazine bag. The only prize I had enough certificates for was a small ball glove that looked more like an overstuffed mitten than a big leaguer's mitt. A salesman's life was not for me. I guessed I was going to have to go back to mowing lawns and pray for an early snow.

A School Day

Bill Heyduck

THE SCHOOL DAY OVER, I left my third-grade class and hurried home.

As I watched other students pass my house, I saw a big sixth-grader knock a first-grader down. Without thinking I charged across the street and yelled, "Leave him alone."

It took a week for my black eye to heal.

Paddling to Canada

Bill Heyduck

MARTY FITZPATRICK WENT TO St. Patrick's grade school and I went to Garfield public grade school, but we both ended up in the same homeroom at Roosevelt Junior High. Marty only lived a block away from me, but since we had gone to different schools we'd never had a reason to really get to know each other. In junior high school, however, we became fast friends.

There was an English teacher we were both very fond of; almost everyone who took her class was fond of Mrs. Conard. She was 5 feet 2 inches of energy and good cheer. She always had encouraging words for everyone and insisted that we all had a special talent buried someplace within us. She was especially vocal in her demand that everyone stand tall and hold their heads up high. Much of this was aimed at the girls. She would say that just because girls tended to be taller than boys at this age there was no reason for them to slouch. Miss Conard loved poetry and read it to us at every opportunity. She didn't just read it, she filled it with emotion, so much emotion that we didn't just hear the words, we felt them.

It was 1942, the first year of World War II, and she picked a lot of patriotic poems to read. One poem was so emotionally charged I can remember parts of it today. I think it was titled "The Hell Gates of Soissons"—at least that's how it sounded to my eighth-grade ears. The pictures I created from the words still remain in my mind today of the twelve brave English soldiers crawling, one after another, through a hail of bullets to their deaths. They tried to light the fuse of explosives to blow up a bridge in order to halt a German advance during World War I. I could hear the bullets zipping by my head and see the flashes from the German rifle barrels as she read us the poem.

Miss Conard also spoke French and slipped French words in occasionally to add color to some of her descriptions of everyday activities. The idea of being able to communicate in a foreign language encouraged me and Marty to stay after school and beg Miss Conard to teach us French words. Each week we tried to memorize and learn how to pronounce three or four words. We thought that in a few weeks we would know enough to converse on the telephone in French and impress our families. I'm afraid that being able to say hello, how are you, good-bye, and knowing the names of the seven days of the week didn't lead to a very interesting conversation.

There was another reason why we wanted to learn to speak French; we had great plans to go to Canada after high school graduation and become fur trappers. We understood that in Canada you could homestead land and after two years, it was yours to keep. We knew where Canada was, but we didn't know much about the culture. We thought almost everyone in Canada spoke French. All the Canadian mountain men and fur trappers we had read about had been French. We had immersed ourselves in books by James Fennimore Cooper; tales about the exploits of Jim Bridger, the mountain man; and anything about Indians we could find.

We spent many afternoons stretched out on the floor of Marty's house going through catalogs, picking out the proper clothes, traps,

Le Canada ou le buste !

rifles, and tools we would need get started in the fur trapping business and to build our first cabin. We didn't want to be slip-shod in our planning because once we got to the north woods, it would be hard to get supplies. We planned everything down to the finest detail. We were going to buy all of our equipment in the United States before we left for our trip north. Blame it on our young age for failing to see this was a real fault in our plans. Why would anyone in his right mind buy all this stuff and lug it all the way to Canada when it could easily be purchased much closer to the destination? Not only would we have all this equipment, but we planned to load it in a canoe on the Mississippi River and paddle it all the way to Canada. A closer reading of the map would have shown us that the Mississippi River ended in Minnesota, not Canada. Not realizing this, we continued our planning throughout the school year.

Near the beginning of ninth grade, we started having guidance classes to help us prepare for the subjects we would need to take in high school, aimed at our future employment goals. The guidance teacher started around the room asking different students if they had decided what they wanted to do after high school. The first girl wanted to be a nurse, so the guidance counselor suggested she take a lot of science courses to prepare for nursing school. The next student wanted to work with his father as a sheet-metal worker, so vocational metal classes were his suggested direction. When the teacher got to me, I stood up and said I was going to be a fur trapper. The teacher looked at me in mild shock for a moment, then smiled and said she would put me down for a college preparatory schedule of classes just in case I changed my mind later.

After ninth grade, Marty started high school at St. Teresa and I started at Stephen Decatur High. As a result of our separation, Marty and I drifted apart and seldom saw each other. Our boyhood dream of fur trapping in Canada slowly faded away as boyhood dreams sometimes do. Adulthood loomed ahead of us. Sometimes at night when I am away from the noise of the city and I hear the tree frogs singing and the owls hooting, I wonder what the sounds of the Canadian wilderness would have been like.

Bill Heyduck

I WAS BORN in Centralia, Illinois, but grew up in Decatur, Illinois. Eight days after I graduated from Decatur High School, I joined the United States Marine Corps. After my discharge from the Marines, I enrolled at Millikin University, graduating with a BA in Art. That summer I was hired as the television scenery designer for WTVP in Decatur. In August I left the television job and headed for Mexico to start an MFA program at Mexico City College. While in Mexico, I worked on weekends as a scenery painter at XEL Televcentro.

After receiving my MFA, I returned to Illinois and started teaching art in the public schools. While teaching, I received a second master's degree from the University of Illinois. I taught art in the public schools for twelve years and then got a teaching job at Eastern Illinois University where I taught ceramics in the art department for twenty-nine years. After starting work at Eastern, I completed a DEd in art education from Penn State and started a ceramic business.

After retiring from Eastern, I took a course in memoir writing. I got the writing bug and haven't stopped. I am now writing fiction as well as a memoir.

I have been married to the same woman for fifty-nine years, and I have two grown children and four grandchildren.

Forgotten Memory

Madeline Ignazito

There are memories we choose to forget, but they keep filtering through our consciousness, stroking the core of our being. We remember again. And again.

During the last few weeks, the past came back resoundingly, namely because of the political assaults on women.

My story is hardly a tragedy but certainly exemplifies the proverbial brick walls we are confronted with in our lifetimes.

One cold November day I was walking home from my piano lesson. I was fourteen and a sophomore in high school. Twice a week I would walk from high school to my teacher's home, which was not far from the school. It was a beautiful part of town with lovely homes and yards nicely planted. My hometown of Long Branch had both an uptown and a downtown business area. The uptown area was literally up, as it was on a hill that rose from the downtown area. Usually I would take the uptown bus to the downtown area and transfer to the bus that took me straight home.

That fateful day I decided to save my bus money and walk down the avenue. I had all kinds of savory plans for that money. I loved candy bars, especially chocolate, and to have money to buy one was a luxury. I loved walking and looking at the big houses along Broadway Avenue that were set back from the road. The homes had stairways leading up to the front doors. They were majestic—I imagined living in such a home.

I was casually walking on the south side of the avenue with my book bag of music and books and an umbrella. It was cold out and I was wearing a bulky aqua-colored winter coat. The coat reached down to below my knees. It was not fitted but flared from the neck down.

As I was trekking along, I noticed some young boys on bicycles coming up beside me. They braked and put their bikes in the gutters of the road. They looked at me and then at each other, nodding with a smirk on their faces. I had no idea what they were up to, but I instinctively began to walk a little faster. There was no one around except an older lady across the street and down the road, so I felt somewhat safe.

All of a sudden one of the boys somehow got in front of me and was rolling on the ground in front of and toward me. He reached his arm under my coat and touched me. I was scared and immediately sat on the ground, wielding my umbrella. I started screaming but the old lady just looked and did nothing. They warned me that if I told my father they would take me to a field, pointing to one down to the right. I was very naive and had no idea what they were talking about. Finally they left and I scurried across the street and continued down the avenue, crying and very upset. How I wished I had taken the bus. Walking across the railroad, I walked right past the police department. I was so traumatized I wanted to get home where I would be safe so I kept going. I kept running and running through town. Not one person stopped to find out what was wrong.

My mom knew something was wrong and persuaded me to tell her what happened. She called the police, explaining the incident to them. The policeman wanted to talk to me. He asked if I knew the boys. I explained that they were younger and I had never seen them before. I could tell by the way he talked to me that he did not believe me. In a sneering and insinuating manner, he kept insisting that I must have known them from school. I started to cry and handed the phone to my mother. He asked her if I would come down to the station to look at their books of suspects. I decided not to go, as his tone of voice was frightening. So I said no. And so it ended. My one regret is that those boys may have gone on to do even more harm, and I had given them a ticket to do so.

Windows

Madeline Ignazito

I

It's the crispy time of the year—leaves stomped on and broken apart
Cooler temperatures, more energy.
The walnuts, ever my nemesis, keep falling on the roof
Sometimes taking me by surprise in the middle of the night.
They are more numerous than the leaves—
One must walk carefully.
Slowly the leaves continue to fall
Leaving a skeleton of branches and trunks against the sky.
Slowly the woods open up, allowing me to see into the ravine.
The deer who are always there are more likely to be seen now
Going up and down the hills, sometimes running playfully.
Eboneezer, our black cat, moves more slowly now
Finding warm places to sit. Just as I do.
A temporary adagio with a long diminuendo into winter
When all will seem tranquil and still in the woods
A time of contemplation, a thinking time,
A time to be quiet and still.

The Memory Pool

II
Beyond the pane moonlight streams through the trees
Myriad patterns striking the darkened grasses
Glistening dew reflecting lunar streams of light
Silence interrupted by a guttural bark
Reddish fur gleams strikingly beautiful
A tail, long glossy fluffy
Barks heard again. Then
More barking more strident from a larger red fur being
Looking out the doorway of its doorway
But never putting a foot outside.
The fox looks and barks again and runs off.
The red setter now with much courage runs out
Seemingly chasing the fox away.

Madeline Ignazito

ON THE ATLANTIC Coast is my hometown of Long Branch, New Jersey. There I obtained both a BMUS and an MMUS in piano performance and composition, studying piano with Jacob Lateiner and composition with Arnold Franchetti.

I have taught music on every level from preschool to college teaching in the music department at Lakeland College. I studied with Hubert Kessler and was honored to play both his compositions and my own for his memorial at Smith Hall, the University of Illinois in Champaign.

In 1981 our family moved from Champaign to Charleston, Illinois. I became president and cofounder of Charleston-Mattoon Music Teachers. I also served on the Coles County Arts council as music director twice and as president. I founded the Honors Recital, which has given over a hundred music camp scholarships to talented students from the area. *My Variations and Fugue* for Chamber Orchestra won a national first prize. I was honored to write the score for the play *Alchemies* by David Radavitch, presented by the Charleston Alley Theater in collaboration with a film artist at Tarble Arts Center, Eastern Illinois University.

My newest work, *Windows*, is a septet written for piano, string quartet and bass, flute and bassoon. It premiered in March for the one hundredth anniversary of a music group in Champaign-Urbana, Illinois. I also wrote two poems titled "Windows" to accompany the music.

I have been active in Illinois State Music Teachers Association as part of a committee writing the Achievement in Music theory tests for the state and also as State Theory Chair for five years.

My husband and I live in a solar house in the country where we raised two daughters, now married with children of their own. Our four grandchildren are the joy of our life.

I have been writing poetry and music since childhood. Music is poetry and poetry is music.

More Blessed to Give
Than to Receive

✠

Helen Krehbiel-Reed

In my childhood home, Christmas traditions included lots of baking, eating, singing, and church programs. The most important tradition, however, was that the family stay together for Christmas Day. We would open the single gift each of us received in the morning and later enjoy a bountiful Christmas dinner. Even after my older brothers and sisters left home, woe to anyone who interfered with the Zerger plan. The in-laws could find another day!

Gene and I tried hard to satisfy the requests of the two sets of grandparents who wanted us to help them enjoy Christmas. After several years of traveling with three children, and lots of lost toys, stress, and upheaval, we decided to start our own traditions. The most important one would be to stay home and open gifts together early, then have Christmas dinner together.

One beautiful fall Sunday after church and Sunday School, Tim, my oldest son, announced, "Mom and Dad, this year I've decided that I don't want any Christmas gifts. I'm going to give all my presents to an eleven-year-old boy at Kemmerer Village." My husband

and I were quite surprised by this announcement, but we looked at each other and beamed with pride, thinking, "What a special child we've got here!" We assumed he was learning important lessons from Rev. Cliff. I was sure Tim would change his mind but thought it was wonderful he was taking the Bible to heart, especially the verse "It is more blessed to give than to receive." It was rewarding to know he was so mature at the age of eleven.

Every week Tim would remind us that he did NOT want any Christmas gifts and that he wished to give them all to a child less fortunate. I listened, nodded, and thought, "Yeah, right! Listen, little guy, you will have at least one Christmas present if I have anything to say about this!" I was pleased to help him fulfill his wishes about sharing his Christmas, but I was still waiting for him to change his mind. And even if he didn't, I would give him a gift or two anyway.

Tim came home from Sunday School one day with a list from Rev. Cliff, who had received it from Kemmerer Village. Included were the items most needed by the children in the orphanage: mittens, earmuffs, scarves, caps, and warm socks. How much fun is that? Well, I guessed I could just buy two of everything and give Tim one set and add some games he might like.

The day came for us to go shopping. Tim and I went off to town with the list in our hands. We bought all the items, and Tim decided he wanted to give the child a game, too — either Connect Four or Parcheesi.

I made sure I kept track of what we bought and what Tim liked, and hoped to come back and buy those things I wanted him to have. The deadline was approaching for the gifts to be transported to the orphanage in time for Christmas. Tim and I wrapped and placed them in a box, then wrapped the box and labeled it "For Boy Age 11."

As Christmas approached, Tim reminded me often that he meant what he said about not wanting any gifts. Well, now really, I was the mother and he was the kid. If it weren't for that Rev. Cliff, none of

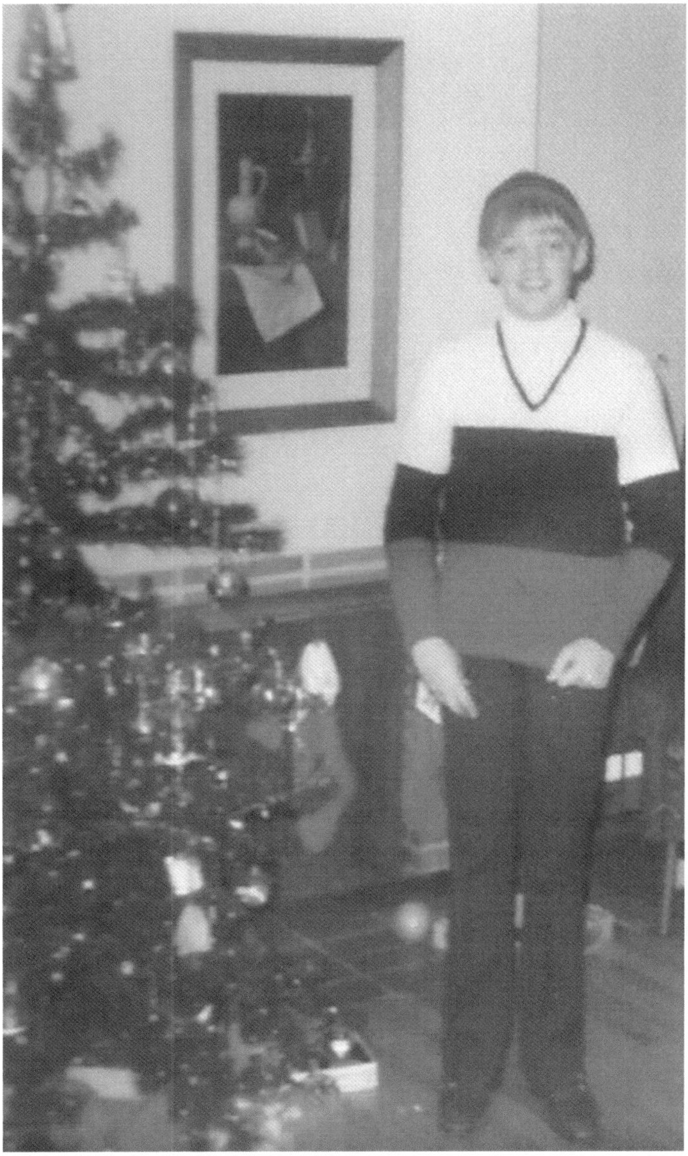

this would be going on. He was truly meddling in my tradition business! He should have known that Tim had two younger brothers. How would it seem to them to get gifts from Santa, Mom and Dad, and Grandma, and then notice that Tim didn't get anything? They might suffer great emotional damage if I let that happen. And what about Tim? He would certainly suffer if there were no gifts for him under that tree on Christmas morning!

Aha—Grandma! There was my answer! My mom always sent a Christmas check so that I could decide what to get for the boys. My scheme was to use her entire check on Tim's gift and say it was from his grandmother. What a good idea! Anyway, Tim would never know how much money Grandma had included for him, and the other boys wouldn't notice anything was awry. If this didn't work out, maybe we'd have to change churches. What if my other boys followed Tim's example? My traditions would be completely ruined!

I proceeded with my plan to spend Grandma's money for Tim's gifts that year. He got a Connect Four game and a few articles of clothing, which I wrapped in one big box and put "From Grandma" on it—no Santa, no Mom and Dad. What a cool plan!

Christmas morning arrived. Why was I so stressed out? I kept telling myself it would all turn out just fine. The kids got up early as usual. They came bounding out of their beds, streaking for the living room and the presents under the tree. Was it my imagination or was Tim less enthusiastic than usual on Christmas morning? I was feeling smug, thinking I had handled the situation masterfully, and I hoped that Tim would be excited as well about his gift from Grandma.

But my bubble burst rather quickly when he spied a gift meant for him. He put his hands on his hips and said, "I told you I didn't want any gifts this year! Why didn't you listen to me?" I had no answer. I truly wished I had listened to him! Oh, how I wished I had! I was only trying to do the right thing. Who would have guessed that he would stick to his idea all the way through Christmas morning?

In my faded recollection of that moment, I believe that Tim did open his gift and even wrote his grandmother a thank-you note for all those presents in the box. As for me, I was brought to a new reality, one in which a youngster can begin his tradition of giving in his own way. It didn't have to be introduced and carried out by his mother.

To this day, Tim's gifts to me are of the alternative variety: a goat for the Heifer Project or disaster relief money given in my honor. I'm proud to say Tim did teach me that it is truly "more blessed to give than to receive." Tim also taught me the lesson that a mother doesn't have the right to try to change a youngster's mind about Christmas giving, particularly when he learned his lesson from Rev. Cliff and the Bible!

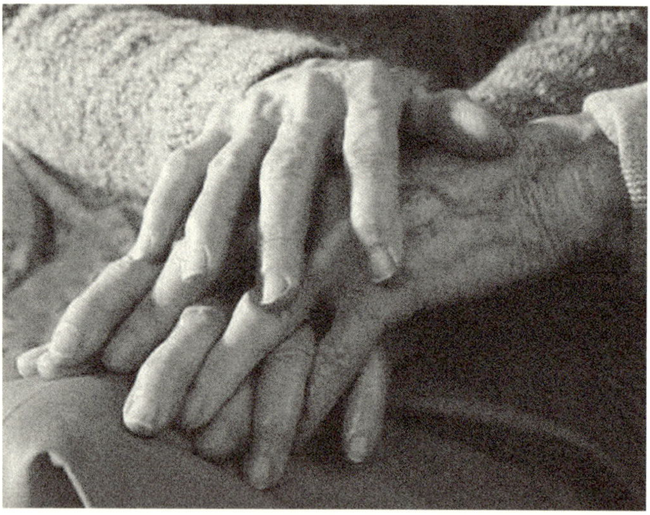

Love and Marriage

Helen Krehbiel-Reed

LATE IN LIFE
Love and marriage
Lucky to find someone so dear and kind
Larger-than-life personality
Loved by friends and family
Loyal to a fault
Lots of adventures, travels, birthdays, anniversaries
Lots of up times, few downers
Link two families together happily
Live together amicably

DEATH!

Lost everything except millions of happy memories

Helen Krehbiel-Reed

My hometown is Moundridge, Kansas, where I was raised on a farm, the fifth child of six. I attended a one-room school named Peaceful, followed by Moundridge High School, then four years at nearby Bethel College. I have taught both public school music and elementary classrooms in Kansas and Illinois.

After the death of my first husband, I returned to the University of Illinois and completed a doctorate, which led me to the position of professor of music education at Eastern Illinois University. I enjoyed teaching at all levels. I am now retired and enjoy traveling to visit my three sons and their wives and families.

My first love is music, and I enjoy the challenge of performing piano duets with a dear friend in the Charleston, Illinois, area. Other hobbies include playing bridge, writing, reading, and sewing. I enjoy and appreciate my wonderful friends while I mourn the recent loss of my husband, John.

Happy Trails

Amy Lynch

The summer of 1991, Erin turned six and had just finished kindergarten in Missoula, Montana. Kyle was three, and our family was on the move. My twelve-year-old niece and nine-year-old nephew were visiting and we needed to make a 700-mile drive to Rapid City, South Dakota, where Doug would drop us off before continuing on to Florida.

Erin and Kyle had happily driven insane distances their whole lives and looked forward to trips with their lidded cake pans full of paper and crayons that doubled as desks. They loved listening to the books on tape that I'd dubbed from copies at the library. We had a boom box we roped to the dashboard so they could hear the tape in the backseat, and they'd happily color and look out the window while listening to *The Secret Garden* or *Rabbit Hill*.

We planned to put Heidi, Erin, and Eric into the back seat with the dog. Doug chained Kyle's car seat to the seat anchors between the two front bucket seats, which worked fine and gave him a good view as long as he didn't swing his feet and kick the car out of gear!

As our departure day got closer, I started to have some qualms. How could I avoid thirteen hours of "Are we there yet?" and "She's squishing me. I need more room!"

Time was incredibly tight and we couldn't dawdle to make the trip more enjoyable. We needed to get there in just one day. My solution was a simple one: bribery with candy. The concept was completely foreign to our normal sets of rules, but this trip had to get us there in one piece and let us arrive with everyone in good spirits for a family wedding in a few days time.

I explained the rules in advance to all four kids. For every hour that no child complained, all of the children would earn a quarter. Each time we stopped, they could spend all of the money they'd earned on anything they liked, including candy. Erin and Kyle were amazed and Heidi and Eric were intrigued. It got us off on the right foot, and that gave Heidi and Eric time to get into the groove of this kind of travel.

Our kids were good travelers. Erin was a great storyteller and a whiz at memorizing the lyrics of old camp songs, and Kyle, who was a hesitant speaker, was happy to follow her lead, repeating what she'd said, often with his own twist. The older kids, with an eye on the finances, jumped in to distract and cheer everyone up before I could declare any hour a "grouchy one." They greeted Kyle's repeated, "Hey guys! Look at that!" with cheerful agreement. "That IS a big truck. What color is that?" And they happily handed his stuffed dog Dada to him over and over as it "fell" into the back seat. Instead of disappearing into their own books and magazines, they learned the words to a lot of very silly songs to sing with Erin. From the front seat I could see their eyes meet over her head a few times as they'd grin while belting out, "She sailed away on a bright and sunny day on the back of a crocodile."

We arrived in Rapid with everyone in good spirits and saw Doug off early the next morning on the rest of his trip. I'm sure that car felt twice as big, but awfully quiet.

For the next few days, the kids and I helped with the wedding preparations but took lots of breaks for the kids to visit Dinosaur Park and take walks through the fields behind my mother's house, the kids and dog circling like electrons while my mother and I guided them toward the park. Halfway there we'd cross a small bridge over Rapid Creek, and they'd spend a few minutes dropping sticks off one side and running to the other to shout their stick along.

The wedding went beautifully and the next morning Erin, Kyle, and I boarded a plane to fly down to meet Doug, just in time for his birthday. As I settled Kyle into his seat and jiggled my backpack under the seat in front of him, Erin sat up as straight as she could in her window seat, barely able to see above the window's bottom edge. She conscientiously found her seat belt and let me reach over to shorten one strap before she carefully latched it in place. She felt uneasy riding without her booster seat. Both children would have had better views if I could have had them both in car seats, but traveling alone I had no arms to spare. Kyle, at three, was even smaller in his seat and had no chance to see the view out the window. The flight attendant down the aisle was speaking and Erin strained to listen, though she couldn't see her from where she sat.

"Mom, are we blasting off yet? Do we have oxygen masks? Where? Up there? That's where they stay? That's where the oxygen comes? OK. We're blasting off!"

She was a bundle of nervous energy. Not quite worried, but very alert and a little anxious as the engines started to rumble under us. Kyle was tired and unhappy, having missed his nap, and he began to make unhappy sounds to himself. Erin, always tuned into his moods, began to talk to him and I lay back in my seat, glad to be sitting still.

"Kyle, it's OK. That is just the sound of the engines. It will be stopping soon." Then, as she reconsidered, she modified her approach, "Well it might take a little while before that noise is over. Here we go. This is exciting. Aren't you excited? Sometimes it is scary. I was a little nervous a long time ago when I blasted off. Do you want a lollypop? Mom, Kyle wants a lollypop. Oh, this is so exciting. Oh, we are almost going to blast off. I better hold on tight."

"Eee, eee, eee," squirmed Kyle, not understanding the motion as he was pushed back against the seat cushions by the force of the plane's speed down the runway. I pulled out a book from the backpack and began an animated rendition of Harold and the Purple Crayon, and succeeded in distracting Kyle from his concern.

"Ah, this is it," Erin chortled as the nose of the plane rose, tipping us all even further back into our seats. "We are in the sky," she sang out and I heard a few people behind us murmur it softly to themselves. "We are in the sky..." drawing the word out the way Erin had.

Once the plane leveled out, the trip was similar to every car trip we'd ever taken. I paced out the entertainment: a book, then a pause while the kids talked to each other or looked around. Then, when I heard a sigh, or Kyle started to frown, I'd rummage about in the backpack and pantomime surprise and delight as I found finger puppets or oranges or tablets and red crayons, doling them out in a measured way to keep things from being too exciting or too boring. We just needed to pass the time and avoid noticing how long everyone had to sit still.

"Oh, what's this? Two tiny packages of raisins! How great. Would you guys like to eat raisins?"

Erin helped Kyle open his box as he repeated happily, "Eat raisins, eat raisins." This routine held up pretty well until they both fell asleep.

Landing in Atlanta, I struggled to get them both up and moving, as Erin was cross on being wakened and Kyle simply couldn't be roused at all. I finally carried Kyle and my backpack off the plane while Erin wobbled at my side. We made it to the next gate and they were awake in time to board. We resumed our routine with Erin helping cheer Kyle along with descriptions of what was going on, and when he got bored, telling him fanciful versions of "Jack and the Beanstalk" and "Goldilocks and The Three Bears." As we got close to Panama City the ride started to get pretty bumpy. Erin was still in the mood to be thrilled.

"Mom! It's a ride. Wheee."

But Kyle was another story.

"No! Get out, get out, get out," and finally, a plaintive, "Sit on lap, sit on lap?"

When the plane made a loud rumble, I told Kyle they were using the flaps to slow the plane down, which reminded him of his toy planes and caught his attention. I had him listen for a noisy thud that would mean they were lowering the wheels and we'd be landing soon.

And then we were down with a bounce and Kyle smiled as Erin patted his hand and said, "We're almost there."

It was dark as we got off the plane and walked down the jetway. Just inside the gate Doug was waiting. I leaned down and whispered in Erin's ear, and she raced forward shouting,

"Happy Birthday Daddy! We are here!!"

Doug bent down to hug them both as Kyle jogged behind, saying, "Birthday, we're here. Birthday, we're here."

Photographs

Amy Lynch

I LOVE PHOTOGRAPHS. I THINK a lot about photographs. I take them obsessively: of birds in my yard, of flowers blooming especially well, of friends over for a party, and of grown-ups reading stories to children who are lost in thought beside them. The urge to capture those images, to freeze that lovely moment in time, to crystallize all the emotions I feel into 1000 pixels is a compulsion and one my family is relatively willing to tolerate. But is it really possible to put time in a bottle that way? I think so.

I have an old picture that seems to convey such a captured moment in time almost ninety years ago. It must have been taken in 1926 and shows my frowning father sitting on the shoulders of his Uncle Frank. They are outdoors in a tidy yard. Frank is young and happy, his large hands holding my father's feet securely against his chest. My dad looks serious, not worried about his perch, but not light of heart. Who was the photographer, and what did he or she feel as that picture was snapped?

Depending on the date it was taken, it may have been my grandfather, taking a picture of his son with his wife's youngest brother in a moment of casual relaxation. My dad's frown could be a result of an interrupted nap. But if taken a few months later, maybe my grandmother, a new widow, with a two-year-old son and an eleven-year-old daughter and no means of support, snapped the picture. Was she taking a last roll of film before the camera was sold? In that case my father's frown could be that of a boy whose world has tipped on end. Maybe she was looking through that viewfinder and seeing not her kid brother, but the uncle she hoped would help her young son learn to be a man, now that his own father was gone. (If so, I hope she was reassured.)

My dad had many uncles. His mother was from a large German Catholic family, and, among them, her brothers did help her raise her children. As a child, my dad worked for a slightly shady uncle who sold fresh fruit on the street and who required that overly ripe strawberries be hidden in the center of the pint. He taught my father ethics inadvertently and helped raise a straightforward and honest man. My father had an uncle who worked for a factory where a company doctor accused the uncle of malingering as he died, on the company grounds, of a heart attack. My father the union man was born. He had Uncle Emil, who married a beautiful and foolish woman but privately advised my dad to marry an intelligent woman, one who could carry on an interesting conversation. My father followed both the example and the advice, marrying my beautiful, intelligent mother. And my father had his Uncle Frank, who is the young man in the picture, and whom he loved and admired regardless of Frank's employment as a bookie.

If I had been born a boy, I was to have been named Frank. As a child, that struck me as an excellent reason to have been born a girl, but now I feel conscious of the blessing that would have been bestowed along with the name of the beloved uncle. I have in my home a painting signed by Frank. It is a fading watercolor of roses, beautifully framed.

So I know Frank was also an artist, a trait that sadly did not get passed on to his nephew or his nephew's children!

So if it was my grandmother taking that picture, I'm sure that as she studied her brother and her son, she knew everything would be all right. She would have seen the love and support her family would give her and know that with their help, things would work out. Maybe she'd even imagined the day in the future when Frank would stand up as best man for Ed at his wedding, sending him off on his new life, still centered around family and filled with the joy that comes from taking care of each other. The life I was fortunate enough to share.

I love photographs.

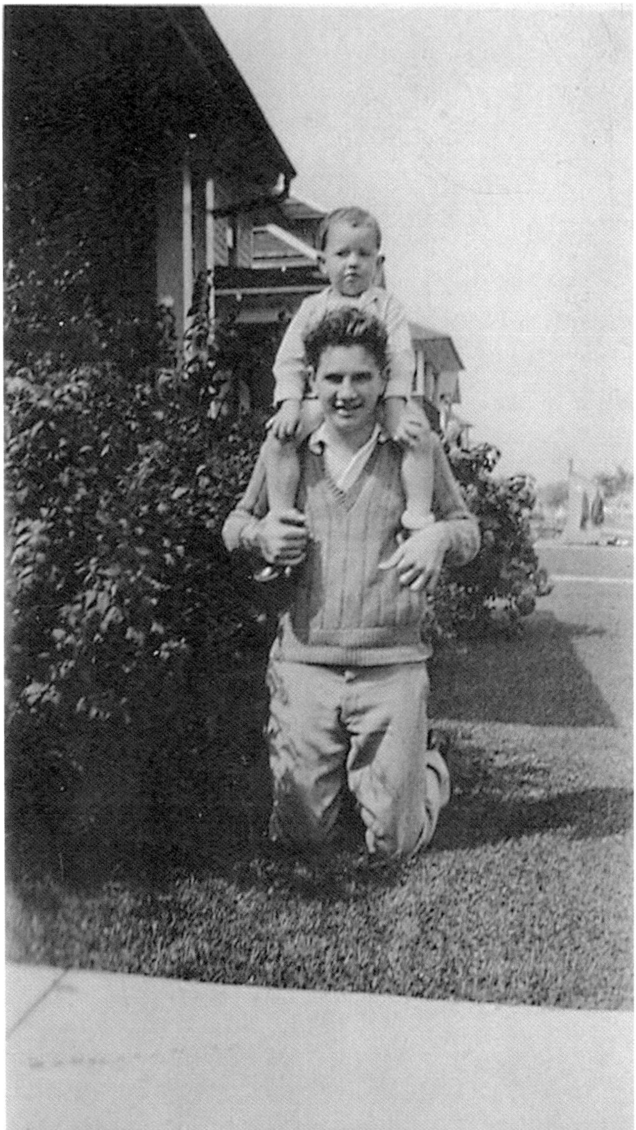

Amy Lynch

I live in Charleston, Illinois, with the best guy I know, my wonderful husband Doug Klarup and our little dog Elf. Doug and I both work at Eastern Illinois University. Our daughter Erin Jean Lynch-Klarup lives and works in Washington, D.C., and our son Kyle Edward Lynch-Klarup is studying physics at the University of Oregon in Eugene.

I had a great stroke of luck when I fell in with this marvelous crowd of creative and talented writers. The stories we share with each other enrich all of our lives and we have so much fun being together that I am amazed to discover how much we are accomplishing at the same time. Without this group I would never have put any of my stories down on paper. With the guidance of the spectacular Daiva Markelis and the inspiration of writers like Lee Isaacson Roll and Jane Cavins Gilbert, I've written down these snippets and impressions from the past and discovered as I did so that they illuminated many other memories I had almost forgotten or never understood. Writing with this group has given me a chance to share these stories with my family and now with some of you. It has been a joy and a privilege, and I am grateful.

A Hair-Raising Experience

Janet Messenger

"We need to do something about that hair of yours," Mom said. "It's so long that all the natural curl is gone. Now that you're twelve years old and about to enter junior high school, you'll be involved in lots of activities, so let's do something to make it easier for you to manage your hair. I think a permanent is the answer. It'll give your hair the body it needs and you can try different hairstyles."

"Okay," I said, thinking that would be great. Now I could try all the new hairstyles I saw in *Seventeen*, my favorite magazine.

Mom picked up the telephone, called the beauty shop and made an appointment for the permanent. She smiled as she hung up the phone and said, "You're in luck. They have an opening tomorrow morning. I told them we'd be there."

Since this would be my first visit to a beauty shop, I began to fantasize what it would be like. I imagined the salon would be located on a busy street downtown and when I walked in the front door I'd be greeted by bright lights and smells of perfume, and everything would be sleek and modern. I'd be seated in a swivel chair in front of a large round mirror framed with lights, a cape would be draped around my shoulders just like in the pictures I'd seen in *Seventeen*, and a stylish beautician wearing a colorful smock would comb and brush my hair before she started the permanent. I was sure this would be one of the most memorable days in my life, one I would remember forever.

How right I was about remembering the experience, but for reasons other than I had expected.

I thought Mom had the wrong address of the beauty shop when we pulled into the gravel driveway of a white house tucked away in the older part of town. This was definitely not the beauty shop in the busy downtown business district I had imagined, nor was it modern and sleek. The house was small and tired-looking. Paint was chipping off the green shutters and a vine with purple flowers was desperately clinging to the siding. A hand-lettered sign reading Gladys's Beauty Nook was staked in the tall grass in the front yard. A large red arrow attached to the bottom of the sign pointed to a narrow uneven cement sidewalk on the side of the house that led to the front door. A cardboard sign that read OPEN—Welcome—Come In was taped to the door.

Inside was one large room, once a sun porch, now converted into the salon. The walls were painted a rosy pink and the floor was covered in a brown patterned linoleum, worn in spots from foot traffic. Two beauty stations, each with swivel chairs, were located in front of two large plain mirrors attached to the wall. On the opposite side of the room were two more chairs with hair dryers attached to the chair backs. I thought they looked like salad bowls turned upside down.

A woman, older than my mother, sat under the dryer engrossed in the pages of a movie magazine while Gladys, the beautician, wielded a rat-tail comb, picking at strands of hair as she put the finishing touches on another lady's hairdo. Perhaps it was the lighting, but I thought that lady had an odd bluish tint to her hair.

"Take a seat," Gladys said to us. "I'll be with you in a jiffy."

A nightmarish feeling crept over me as I sat with Mom on the straight-backed chairs near a table piled high with magazines and newspapers.

Everything seemed so old—even the magazines were outdated. I wondered where all the glamorous customers were, the bright lights, the people younger than my mom? My stomach muscles tightened. I realized this was really a small beauty shop, and although Gladys was cheery and pleasant, I wondered if she kept up with the latest hairstyles. I didn't see one *Seventeen* magazine on her reading table.

Just then Gladys called my name and pointed to her beauty chair. "Sit here," she said as she draped a cape around my shoulders. I began to relax as she gently ran a comb through my hair to remove the tangles and complimented me on the rich red highlights in my auburn hair.

"Now what can I do for you today, dearie?" Gladys said.

It was as though the cat had gotten my tongue. I sat silent in the chair as Mom provided an historical account of my hair.

"You know, Gladys," Mom began, "Janet was eighteen months old before she had hair at all, and when it began to grow it came in in tight ringlets. I'd give it a trim now and then, but never cut much off. How I enjoyed making finger curls all over her head. Everyone used to say, 'My, she looks so much like that darling Shirley Temple.' We also braided her hair. Do you think braiding caused the loss of the natural curl? I think she needs her curls back."

"I think a body perm will be the answer to your dilemma," Gladys replied confidently. "I'll shampoo her hair first, give it a trim and then do the perm."

Great, I thought. Let's get started.

I moved to the shampoo area across the room. Gladys told me to lean back in the chair. Suddenly the back of the chair collapsed. I sat upright with a start. Had I done the unthinkable, broken her chair? If I had, I didn't mean to. I was so embarrassed.

Gladys smiled and chuckled. "It's okay, dear, the chair back is supposed to do that. Just lean back and relax while I get my special shampoo. I think you'll like it. It smells like strawberries."

Wow, I thought. I wonder if it's as good as the Halo shampoo I used at home. I knew the Halo advertising jingle by heart. Maybe if I sang it to myself, it would help me relax. Silently I repeated the words: "Halo, everybody, Halo. Halo is the shampoo that glorifies your hair. So, Halo Shampoo, Halo!" Ah, I was beginning to feel a bit better, and Gladys was back with the strawberry-scented shampoo.

The warm water, the sweet smell of strawberries, and Gladys' fingers massaging my head almost put me in a trance. The shampoo billowed up in mounds of suds. "One more rinse with warm water to get all the soap out," Gladys said. "And then we'll be done here. Next we'll trim your hair and start the perm. Sit up straight now so I can wrap a towel around your hair and you can head back to the big swivel chair."

What a relief. I hadn't broken anything, but I still needed to be cautious since everything around there was old.

The hair trim proceeded smoothly and Gladys made certain she cut my hair to the length I wanted.

Now it was time to start the permanent. Gladys sectioned off my hair as though she were laying out a garden to plant rows of lettuce or radishes. Her nimble fingers smoothed the strands of hair and wrapped them around the rollers. She stepped back to check each one, making sure no stray hairs escaped the grasp of the roller.

Gladys disappeared into the storage closet and returned with a small bottle.

"This is the waving lotion and I'm going to dab it on each roller," she said. "Don't be surprised if it feels a little cold on your head." As the lotion was applied, the most awful smell spread throughout the room. What was this stuff? It made my eyes burn and my nose run. I hoped it was not eating my brain!

I was having serious second thoughts about the benefits of a permanent, but I had come this far and there was no turning back. I just wanted the permanent to be over, finished, but what came next was even more frightening.

Gladys wheeled out the permanent wave machine from the darkest corner of the room. This monstrous "thing" resembled an octopus, complete with tentacles. The top was shaped like a dome from which electric cords dangled. As she pushed the machine across the floor, the metal clamps attached to the ends of the cords clanged together, sounding like the tolling of a bell.

Gladys proceeded to attach a clamp to each of the curlers on my head. I was too frightened now to move. The machine was plugged into the wall socket and a low-pitched hum could be heard throughout the room as electricity surged through the cords. A thought passed through my brain: Is this what it's like to be electrocuted? The machine continued to hum and I could feel heat coming through the clamps. I vowed then and there if I lived through this process I would never, ever, ever have another permanent.

Time passed slowly. Finally the timer rang, signaling that the waving process was complete. The machine was unplugged, clamps were removed, and I was set free. Then the curlers were unwound, the waving lotion neutralized, and the solutions rinsed from my hair. I no longer reeked of that awful waving-lotion smell.

I was ushered back to the swivel chair in front of the large mirror, almost afraid to see the final result. Did I get the "body" necessary to help me style my hair? Yes, I did! In fact, I had body and curls, lots and lots and lots of curls.

Gladys finished drying and setting my hair. I was pleased with the final results as I walked out the door of the salon. Prouder yet that I had survived this experience.

A week later I washed my hair for the first time following the permanent. I expected it would be simple to wash my hair, dry it, and brush it into the style I desired. To my dismay, once washed it turned to frizz. Crying, I ran downstairs to show Mom what the permanent had done — it had ruined my life!

Mom reassured me all would be well, but I still needed to roll my hair in curlers or pin curls to set the style.

As time went on, things improved, but I never went back to Gladys's Beauty Nook. One hair-raising experience was enough.

Old Blue Eyes

Janet Messenger

This morning during my walk my favorite neighbor, Bill, came up to me, cradled my head in his hands, patted me on the head and said, "Well, Milo, old boy, good to see you. It's been awhile, hasn't it?" He scratched behind my ears, then looked me straight in the eyes: "Oh my, it looks like you're having some trouble with your vision these days. I see you've developed cataracts in both eyes. Cataracts aren't that bad though, Milo. I had them myself. The world looks different all right, even fuzzy at times. Now those sparkly brown eyes of yours have turned a frosty blue. I'll have to start calling you Old Blue Eyes like Frank Sinatra. Ha, ha."

We may not have seen each other for a while, but how could he be so confused?

Nothing Bill said made any sense: Old Blue Eyes, Frank somebody or other, cataracts. If his words hadn't shocked me so, I would have said, "No, man, it's me, Milo. You know, I live two houses away from you, little white dog, full of pep, barks early in the morning at the squirrels. Why, you even paid me a compliment once and said

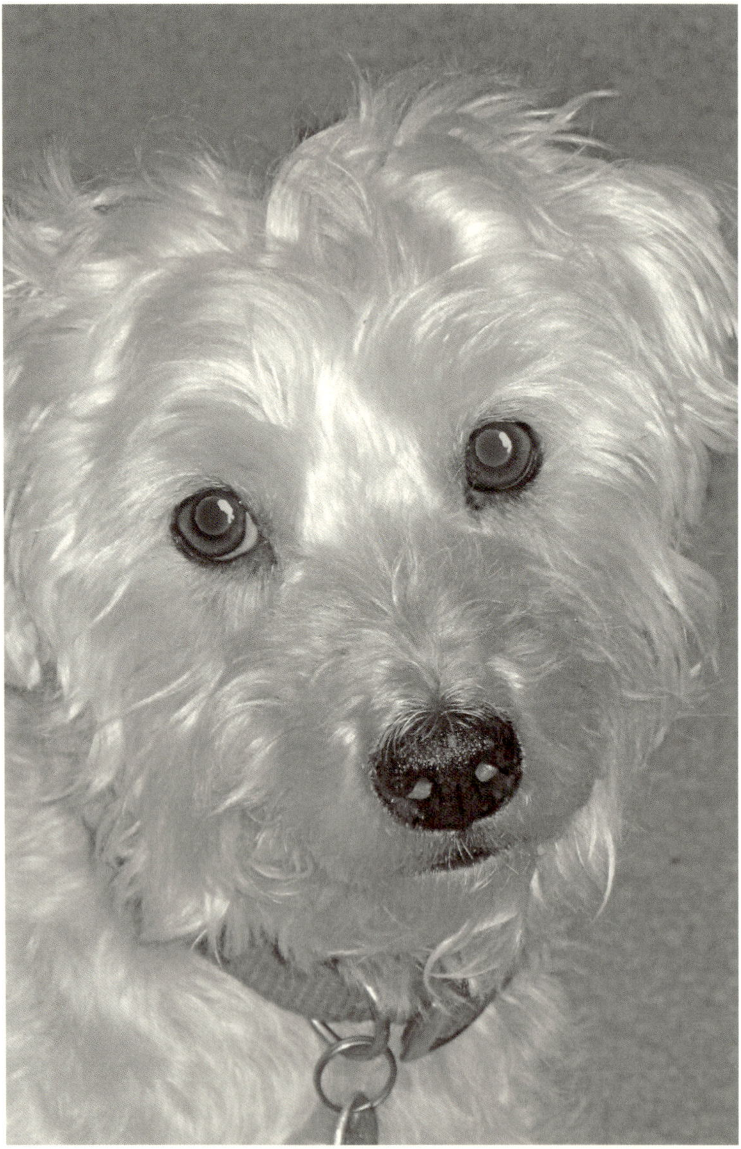

I was just like your 'dagnamet' alarm clock. That Milo, and now you think I'm Frank whomever, that my eyes are blue, I've developed cataracts, whatever they are, and I'm old." What a way to start the day.

I never wished so hard in all my life that a walk would be over. I had to get home in a jiffy to look in the mirror and check things out. "Old Blue Eyes, humph!" I said to myself as I raced up the stairs, my leash hop, skip, and jumping behind me, headed for the full-length mirror at the end of the hall. I had to see for myself if my eyes had changed color. Surely Bill was confused. Poor guy, he'd probably been working in the yard too long and suffered some kind of brain hiccup. Or maybe his tinted eyeglasses were playing tricks on him.

I got as close to the mirror as I could and stared at myself. "No! It can't be," I gasped. My eyes really are BLUE! A little foggy, but blue. Wait, maybe it was just the dim light here in the hall or maybe the mirror was dirty. I took a deep breath, blew on the glass and wiped it with my furry paw, but no matter how much I huffed and puffed or wiped and polished the mirror, the fact remained—my brown eyes were BLUE!

Okay, so Bill wasn't completely bonkers, but what about the other things he said?

My eyes had developed, oh, what was that word? Cadillacs. No, those are cars.

Caterpillars. No, those are worms that turn into butterflies.

Cataracts—that's it, cataracts, but what's a cataract? Where's the dictionary? I'll look up the definition. Let's see. C-A-T-A-R-A-C-T. Oh, oh, I'm getting bad vibes already.

Any word with C-A-T as the first three letters can't be good. Let's see what Mr. Webster has to say: "A clouding of the lens of the eye or of its surrounding transparent membrane that obstructs the passage of light."

Hmm. Okay. That explains some weird things that have happened to me lately.

The TV pictures have gotten rather blurry, colors aren't as bright as they used to be, and the screen gets so dark at times there's no picture at all, only sound. I thought the TV set was getting old, but maybe the cataracts are playing tricks on me. I wonder what else I've missed out on?

I've bumped into several chair legs, tables, and walls lately, and last night I almost missed Janet's lap when I took a flying leap from the floor to the recliner where she was sitting. I knew her lap hadn't shrunk, but the chair seemed to move. Why, if she hadn't caught me like a football in midair I would have missed the chair completely and landed on the floor flatter than a pancake.

Then there was the mysterious incident involving my floor cushion. One day it was in the napping corner of the living room and the next day—gone!

Disappeared. Nowhere in sight. Somebody moved it and it took me hours of nose-to-the-carpet sniffing to locate it. Thank goodness my sense of smell is still intact.

You don't suppose Bill was right when he called me "old boy," do you? No way. Can't be. I'm Macho Milo and I may be growing older, but I feel young, I think young, and I have too many things to do on my bucket list before I'm OLD.

Janet Messenger

Life was good growing up in the small Iowa town of Muscatine, located on a bend of the Mississippi River south of the Quad Cities. I have vivid memories of a happy childhood, loving family, and being a teenager in the 1950s.

Following my high-school graduation I attended the University of Iowa, studied art, and graduated with a BA in art education.

I met the love of my life, Allen, on a blind date and we married shortly after. I taught art at the junior high level until we started our family. I have two sons and five delightful grandchildren. When my sons were teenagers, I earned an MA in education from Washington University in St. Louis.

We settled in Charleston, Illinois, in 1982. I love the small town flavor of this community, its people, and the many amenities Eastern Illinois University affords the area. I was bitten by the writing bug in 2008 after taking an Introduction to Memoir Writing course for adult learners taught by Dr. Daiva Markelis, professor of creative writing at EIU.

When the class ended, six of us banded together to form the Past~Forward Memoir Writing Group. The Coles County Arts Council became our sponsor. Currently we have two writing groups: I coordinate the day group and Daiva leads the evening sessions. Meetings are held once a month. In 2011 we published our first book, *Occasional Writers*, featuring works by sixteen authors. Today we proudly present *The Memory Pool*, featuring works by twenty-two members.

Bob and Tom

Johnni Olds

Who's that? There's a new man on Sarah's countertop, all sparkly. He's quite proud of his clean, modern, plain white color. What a showoff!

Tired-avocado-colored Bob-Big-Boy-Blender was showing his old-timer age, but he'd been through a lot over the years and wasn't about to let this young whipper-snapper run him off HIS counter.

One day, Sarah decided to make a chocolate-swirl pound cake for her dinner guest, Gregory. Tom-Mix-Master enjoyed displaying his talents to Bob-Big-Boy-Blender. He knew the product would be beautifully marbled and tasty.

Later, Sarah employed Bob to make gazpacho for a first course. Bob was ready, willing, and able to chop tomatoes, onion, and peppers. When the tomato juice was added, along with a squeeze of lemon, the job was complete. Bob boasted of his accomplishment to Tom.

They were both proud and satisfied with their good work. It was then they realized rivalry wasn't the answer at all. They could happily work together. Bob would chop and Tom would blend. They became good buddies after they got to know each other.

That evening was a big success. Bob got a little tipsy as he was mixing margaritas, and Tom felt quite decadent while licking chocolate off the bowl. A good time was had by all, and, by the way, Sarah and Gregory lived happily ever after.

Bus Stop

Johnni Olds

Following my instincts, I sat down by the cute redhead. Her dark green eyes were so inviting. While we talked, she wrote down my e-mail address. I was looking forward to private time with her.

As we approached St. Patrick's, she stood and said, "Well, I'm home." She walked toward the convent.

My heart sank.

Please Help

Johnni Olds

I NEEDED HELP, AND A complete stranger offered his assistance. We didn't talk after the initial meeting. I thought it strange that he ignored me, even though I knew he was discussing my situation with others. Days after briefly meeting Bill, I woke up in St. John's Hospital with a healthy kidney.

Thank you, Bill.

My Special Shoes

Johnni Olds

About a year ago my husband, Glen, read an article in the Champaign-Urbana paper that caught his eye. He knew that my custom-made orthopedic shoes would fit perfectly into the World of Shoes exhibit at the Spurlock Museum at University of Illinois, Urbana. He was right.

After several phone calls and e-mails, we were off to Spurlock. Kim, the woman in charge of putting the show together, was pleased with the gift. She said the shoes were unusual because they were made the old-fashioned way, by hand instead of by machine. We gave Kim permission to cut one of the shoes in half to show and describe the various layers. Next to each pair of shoes would be an explanation of how and why the shoes were made, so it would be both an interesting and educational exhibit.

This pair, my first, was made by Pietro Fonda. He is a true cobbler who started work at thirteen, learning the art of shoemaking from his father in his native Italy. He was raised in a rural area and because of his own foot problems couldn't work in the fields like all his neighbors. He came to the United States over fifty-five years ago, first to New Orleans, then to San Francisco, where mine were made. He carved the inner support from wood and shaped the uppers from deer and buffalo hide. When I showed the finished shoes to my podiatrist, he was impressed by their light weight, considering the amount of support they gave.

Now Pietro is in his eighties and still speaks very little English. His partner, helper, bookkeeper, and protégé, Suzanne, is also his interpreter. They have an apprentice working in the storefront shop at the end of a streetcar line in a quiet San Francisco neighborhood. They are very nice people who enjoy discussing their trade.

Pietro is a devout Catholic and attends Mass three times a day. The church is one block away from his shop and there's a convent there for the Missionaries of Charity, founded by Mother Teresa.

In 1995, Mother Teresa stayed at that church, and Pietro noticed her sandals were frayed. The nuns took the sandals from her bedside while she slept and gave them to Pietro. He worked through the night, and the nuns put the repaired sandals where they had been when Mother Teresa went to sleep. She was pleased upon awakening; Pietro had made her very happy. There was talk of keeping the scraps from her sandals as possible relics if she ever became a saint. I'm proud of the fact that the same wonderful man cobbled shoes for both Mother Teresa and me.

I depend on my shoes from the time I get up in the morning until I go to bed at night. They ease my pain and help with my balance. I am so very thankful for these ugly shoes. I look at them as a fashion statement!

Sometimes at Night

Johnni Olds

S**OMETIMES** **I** **GET** settled in bed and notice his scent.
Tonight I smell nothing.

Sometimes I reach out to cuddle with him.
Tonight his side of the bed is empty.

Sometimes I awake wondering why he's not holding me.
Tonight I miss his big hug.

This, like many others, is a restless night.
It's time to invite my cat to sleep with me.

So much time is spent with him away on business.
Is the paycheck worth the separation?

January 2014

Johnni Olds

THE STORY SO far...

Once upon a time in a green hilly land far, far away called Kentucky, a little girl was born. After living on her family's dairy farm for three years, she moved to small villages in Wyoming, Illinois, and Texas until she was nineteen years of age. Then the big day came for her to venture out into the world, and she made San Francisco her home. After forty years she returned to the Midwest and is currently in the process of living happily ever after.

Her favorite pastimes are visiting nursing homes, being involved in her church, learning to play the dulcimer, and anxiously awaiting the World Series in October when the San Francisco Giants will undoubtedly win the title of World Champions. They won in 2010 and 2012 so it stands to reason this year will be another notch on their bats. Every other year is just fine with this Giants fan!

She has haunting memories of the World Series in 1989, which was called the Bay Bridge Series. An earthquake interrupted the meeting of the two best teams in Major League Baseball and badly damaged the Bay Bridge connecting Candlestick Park and the Oakland Coliseum. After a delay of ten days, the A's swept the Giants—a devastating loss to Giants fans—but the truly unforgettable part of this series was the fact that sisty-three people lost their lives in the earthquake.

That's all (for now).

Afghan

Peggy Perkins

Needles clicking.
Fingers flying.
Yarn knitted.
Afghan vibrant, vivid,
Orange, purple, blue,
Like sunlight reflected off a glacier.
Fringe hanging.
Bed covered.
Nice gift, Grandma.

Clock ticking, ticking, ticking

Needles silent.
Fingers shaking.
Yarn torn.
Afghan pale. Faded,
Brown, dreary blues and reds
Sunlight vampires suck out color.
Fringe tattered.
Bed exposed.
Precious gift, Grandma.

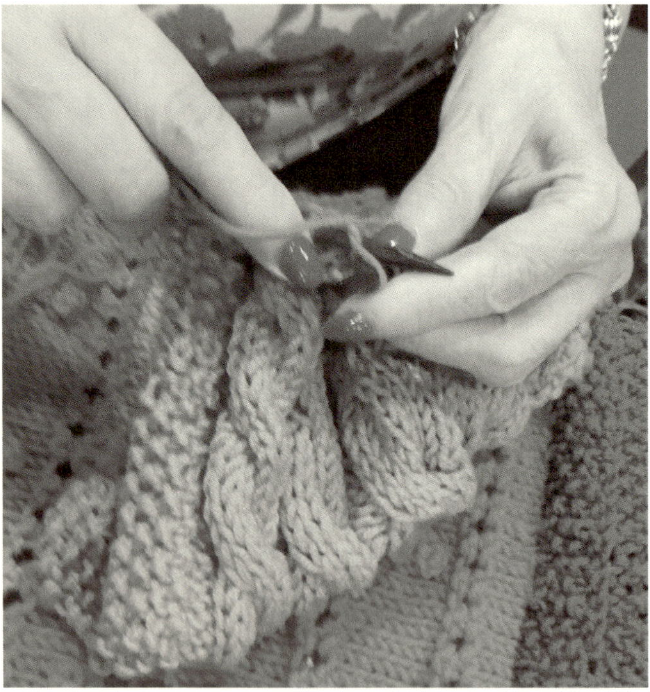

Peggy Perkins

Three years ago, I began my first attempts at memoir. Writing down thoughts and emotions and expressing reactions to past memories resulted in new ideas emerging and feelings returning. I was able to write stories and poems about events I thought were long forgotten. Writing has been a wonderful outlet for my creativity.

Eddie Thompson

David R. Pollard

Tall grasses undulate seductively along fertile fields. Azure sky surrounds the sun. Maximus, magnificent horse, light reddish-brown coat, walks fluidly beneath saddle, blanket, and man. Max has a broad intelligent forehead with keenly alert eyes. His silken flowing light-cream mane descends his muscular chest and angular shoulders. His powerful hindquarters and ground-length tail are supported by sinewy durable legs atop perfectly sound hooves.

A wide-brimmed light gray hat, much like a Stetson Muzzle, though with rounded high crown, rests on the rider's substantial white-haired head. Adequate neck attaches to broad shoulders. Two days growth of white beard contrasts gently with wolf-blue eyes, nose graceful yet otherwise unremarkable.

Rider wears a seersucker suit that is woven in such a way that some threads bunch together, giving the fabric an intermittent wrinkled appearance. The suit is made of thin, puckered, all-cotton light blue subtly striped fabric that allows heat to dissipate and air to circulate.

The rider wears a shirt with a crisply starched collar and a red silk tie. The shirt, originally white, is now a subdued yellow, the result of the gradual build-up of calcium and magnesium from hard water from a very old well for laundry. The man's slight paunch is partially concealed by the ample jacket buttoned once at the mid-section while his pant cuffs are tucked neatly inside Destry working cowboy boots. The rider holds the reins in his left hand to allow the left rein between the ring and middle fingers while the right rein passes between the middle and index fingers. His right arm hangs naturally along the right side, hand slightly below hip. The rider partners perfectly with Max, rocking gently in synchronization with each strong stride. His body language exudes confidence: strong straight posture, relaxed round shoulders. This is Eddie Thompson, retired teacher from agriculture secondary education, accepted by the community as a person peculiar though peaceful, referred to by some as Crazy Eddie, though never with malice. Eddie guides Max gracefully between fields and country roads, as among the heavens.

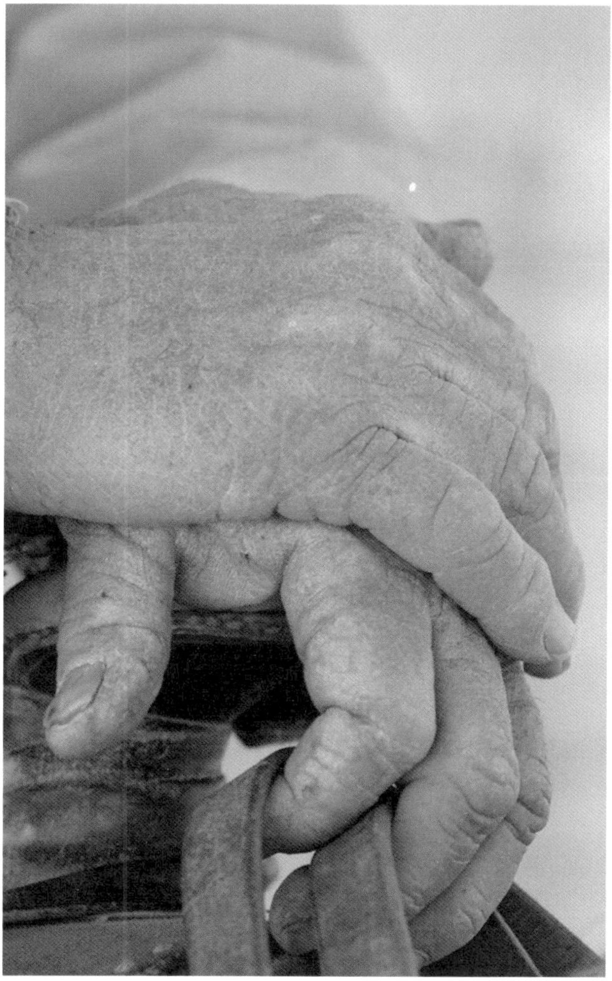

David R. Pollard

Dave has begun to apply pen to paper, thus sharing observations and experiences that for more than half a century were thoughts only. He enjoys a search for the best words to paint a picture for a reader. Some of Dave's Past~Forward fellow writers say that his style is poetic. Dave writes vignettes for the pleasure it brings him, and he is hopeful that others also find comfort therein.

How I Learned to Play Guitar
Off the TV

Julie Rea

Most of us have heard the expression, "Things happen as they are supposed to." Well, in 1965 or so, musical serendipity began to play a role in my life. I was twenty-three with two young children. One evening my then-husband Tom returned home and promptly handed me a $25 Sears guitar. He told me the price right away to keep me from launching into my "We don't have the money" lecture. I was surprised, not recollecting I wanted a guitar. I put guitar and cardboard case aside and went back to washing a sink full of dishes and planning the next meal.

Close to the time I received the guitar that I didn't know how to play, there was another surprise. Tom's father, an army accountant, had picked up a pawnshop reel-to-reel recorder outside Ft. Campbell, Kentucky. The recorder, along with some empty reels, came to us unbidden but not unwelcome in a large box. What a strange turn of events.

I really liked the music of Joan Baez and Buffy St. Marie I'd been hearing on the radio. I had always loved to sing; I'd sung to and with the children since they were born, and now we sang nursery rhymes together every night after story time. Around this same time, I happened to see Laura Weber on WGBH public TV, out of Boston, teaching beginning folk guitar. The program appeared to be just starting. The booklet of guitar chords and folk tunes cost two dollars and fifty cents and would come through the mail.

The next Tuesday evening, I pulled the leather-covered footstool up to the old black-and-white television. I, a budding Joan Baez, was poised and waiting for seven p.m. to start the lesson. I quickly remembered that if a parent was doing something and wanted children to participate, they disappeared. But if an activity looked even a little interesting, they were ready and willing to join in—I had read several child-rearing books by then. Looking around the living room, I grabbed a couple of *Reader's Digest*s from the coffee table, found enough rubber bands, and made my toddlers their very own guitars. Hopefully, they could pretend to play while I tried to follow along with Laura Weber.

The book hadn't arrived yet and there was no getting Miss Weber to stop once she got started to show me that chord one more time! Well, what do you think happened next? Tom connected the reel-to-reel recorder to the TV so I could record the program and replay it as I needed to. Amazing!

We TV guitar students had completed two of the three booklets when Miss Weber announced she would be traveling from Boston to Berkeley putting on hootenannies at various public television stations. Denver would be included, and I was determined to go.

Tom must have agreed I could go and stayed with the kids. Otherwise I wouldn't have had the car. My Sears guitar and I drove down to the television station in Denver. I made a few wrong turns, but I was on Cloud Nine—I didn't get out much by myself. I heard the singing as I raced down the station hall to a large conference room. There, indeed, was Laura Weber way up front, having a grand old hootenanny time. We groupies played along the chords and tunes we had learned from her.

When the hootenanny was over, I waited in line to get an autograph on my dog-eared booklet; the puppy, Molly, had chewed the corner. (The tire tracks across the front cover came much later.)

Anyway, as I was smiling and reaching for my booklet from Miss Weber, I heard a voice behind me. I turned to a little old lady, probably fifty-ish (anyone over thirty seemed old then) with braids on top of her head. Introducing herself as Dorothea Munro, she smiled broadly and asked, "Would you like to come to my house for cocoa?" I thought she was kidding at first, but I followed her anyway, thinking "What am I doing? This is the big city and I'm going to the house of a stranger."

We stopped at the end of a street leading directly into the Japanese Botanical Gardens. The house she lived in beside the gardens with her sister, Prudence, had been built by their father when they were children. While Pru whipped up some cocoa at this late hour, Dorothea showed me around the main floor. The large living room had a fireplace and two overstuffed chairs—a perfect setting for tea. The dining room could barely hold the two baby grand pianos where she and Pru played duets. The dining room table was relegated to a corner of the living room.

After that amazing meeting, Dido, as she liked to be called, and I met at her house or mine weekly to practice and share stories for an hour. We did this till our little family left Denver for Eastern Illinois University in 1967 so Tom could finish his bachelor's degree on the GI Bill. Here we met many other folksinger/guitar pickers. Tom was given a "throwaway" guitar from EIU's Wesleyan Youth Center. He had it repaired and gave it to me. A former seamstress for Chicago rock bands named Sue created a couple of costumes for me. Several of us went on to play functions at EIU's Ratskeller and the yearly Celebration of the Arts.

My children and grandchildren have continued to support me. In fact, my son-in-law picked up guitar in his forties and writes his own songs. And to think that old thing called serendipity could have had such a happy effect on one life. I guess that's why it's called serendipity.

Turquoise and Race Horses

Julie Rea

Once upon a time in Berryville, Virginia, a very young girl with long, dark braids was enjoying the coolest part of the day on her maternal grandmother's (Nana's) front porch. She was dressed in one of her favorite sunsuits, appropriate for a hot, steamy August day. The Blue Ridge Mountains gently sheltered this small Shenandoah Valley town, not far from the bridge that could take you over the Shenandoah River, straight up into those blue mountains.

Little Julie Ann had situated herself against the cool red bricks of the big old house, her legs straight out in front of her on the vast, shady porch. She was a daydreamy child, content to be by herself, surrounded by lilacs and wild roses and hard maple trees on either side of the porch steps. The front porch was her favorite of the three porches around this happy house. It was a place outside where she loved to be—it felt like sitting on a big person's lap. If she just leaned back and got still, she might feel a heart beating. She adored the swing and wicker rockers on one side of the porch, and the glider and cushioned chairs on the other. She also liked all the space she had alone on the porch.

    Satisfied, she looked down at her small wrist where her new shiny silver bracelet lay with its greenish-blue stone in the middle. She moved her wrist around to better admire this new thing her Mama and Daddy had brought her from their recent trip to Dallas, Texas, Daddy's hometown. She liked to run her fingers over the design on either side of the stone. Mama had three silver bracelets, the one in the middle having the same kind of stone as hers. Still twisting her wrist as she caressed her new bracelet, she looked up into the maple trees and began to daydream about the road trip to Charlestown, West Virginia, later that day to see the horseraces. She tried to imagine what colors the horses would be and how fast they could run.

    She heard a red bird in the maples and looked up into the branches. The bird was hidden by the tree leaves, so she looked back down again at her wrist. Her shiny new bracelet was gone! She felt all around her bare wrist as if her bracelet were really there and she just couldn't see it. She quickly looked around on the porch boards — no bracelet! Maybe it had fallen under the porch. The only place she could see down between the porch boards was where the last board sat a little ways from the front of the house. When she put her face close to the house and this narrow space she could feel cool air against her eyes but could only see darkness.

Little Julie Ann could only daydream about the dark place underneath the porch. What else was under there besides dark? Probably Granddaddy Longlegs, or black spiders and webs that could stick to your fingers if you touched them!

Nobody went under that porch. Even if she could talk her Uncle Junior into crawling under there, he couldn't. It was all closed in with latticework and concrete. It should be so easy though, especially since the bracelet must have fallen in right next to the front door, up against the house where she sat.

She had always felt safe and secure in this house and on its porches. Her hands on her hips, she frowned at the porch and then at the house. She also wondered, for a minute, what Mama would do when she found out the bracelet was gone. That was too scary, so she sat back down where she'd been all along and looked out again at the flowering shrubs and tall maples until she was quickly lifted up without a word and carried into the house. She hadn't heard her mother come out the front door. Her face and hands scrubbed, she was marched out to Granddaddy's long black car to go watch those horses run. Nana sat in the front seat with Granddaddy and Mama in the back with Julie Ann. Aunt Betty must have stayed home to watch her baby sister, Diana. Aunt Betty didn't love horses like Mama did.

All the car windows were open on the short trip to Charlestown to catch any cool wind. Mama had brought a coloring book and crayons for Julie Ann. This would be her first and only horserace. When they got inside, she saw there was no space for peaceful daydreaming there. She found herself squashed in the high stands where it was too hot and everybody was too close. She couldn't even see any horses, although she thought she could hear them running. She couldn't color without everybody jumping up and yelling every few minutes. She couldn't do anything but be upset when everybody jumped up around her like that. She might as well have been in the tall, hot weed patch in Nana's backyard, all sticky, knowing Nana was up by the barn, killing a chicken for Sunday dinner. It was that bad!

When they finally got back to the car, Julie Ann was whiny, hot, and sticky. She looked down and saw her crayons were wet and melting in the heat. That made her cry, which made Mama irritable, so she had to stop crying and just sniffle, stick her lower lip out and pout. Nobody even looked at her!

She just wanted to be back on Nana's front porch, cool and quiet, even if she didn't have her bracelet anymore. She never did remember what Mama said when she noticed it was gone. It was just gone.

Epilogue:

Over sixty-five years later, during my yearly road trip to The Valley, I still sit in my car on South Church Street gazing up the long lawn to what used to be Nana's house. The house and porch seem mostly unchanged. One of the maple trees is gone and bright colored plastic toys are scattered by the porch. I will always think, though, that if I could just get somebody to go under that porch and dig around in the right spot, they would find my little turquoise bracelet. I am sure and certain that it is still there, waiting for me. If I had it back, it would lie in a small china dish on a tiny piece of navy blue velvet on my dressing table. It would be so shiny and catch my eye whenever I sat there. And I would remember.

Julie Rea

Born in Winchester, Virginia, in the Shenandoah Valley, I spent half my childhood there as well as in Waynesboro, Pennsylvania—all in view of blue-ridged mountains.

Preteen life and older found me discovering a world beyond those mountains as an army brat. Our family moved around in Germany a few years before I graduated from a southern Virginia high school on the Atlantic Ocean. My fiancé and I married at Langley Air Force Base, moved a few times, and had two children. We came to Illinois from Denver, Colorado.

I recently retired from Sarah Bush Lincoln Hospital as a licensed, clinical social worker. My son Stephen, a contractor, lives in the Sierra Nevada Mountains of California, and I'm a few miles from daughter Shelley, her husband John, and their three boys. My loves are being with family, folk singing with guitar, gardening, reading, being in nature, taking photos, and now writing stories about all the above.

My mother died at almost eighty-eight leaving me a wealth of her memories. I am now fortunate to participate in two life-enriching writing groups, fondly named "Past~Forward." It is a rare treat to be among fellow writers, reading memories and perspectives in our own words. We are lovingly guided and encouraged by our writing teacher, Daiva Markelis, and our own Janet Messenger, who keeps us connected and smiling.

The Love of My Life

Denise Shumaker

It was a sunny day at her apartment when I first saw Buster. He was in her arms. I loved him at first sight. I coveted him daily with thoughts about how I could make him mine.

Suddenly, she left town. The masked Chihuahua became mine. I will never love another as I did Buster.

Sophie

Denise Shumaker

Her gaunt skeletal figure was hidden in the barn's shadow.

"Do you want me?" Sophie's sad, sunken eyes pleaded.

"No," I replied, "You aren't what I had envisioned."

"But you are my last chance!"

I couldn't bear to see her slaughtered. I bought the mare. Now her gold-flecked chestnut coat gleams in the sun.

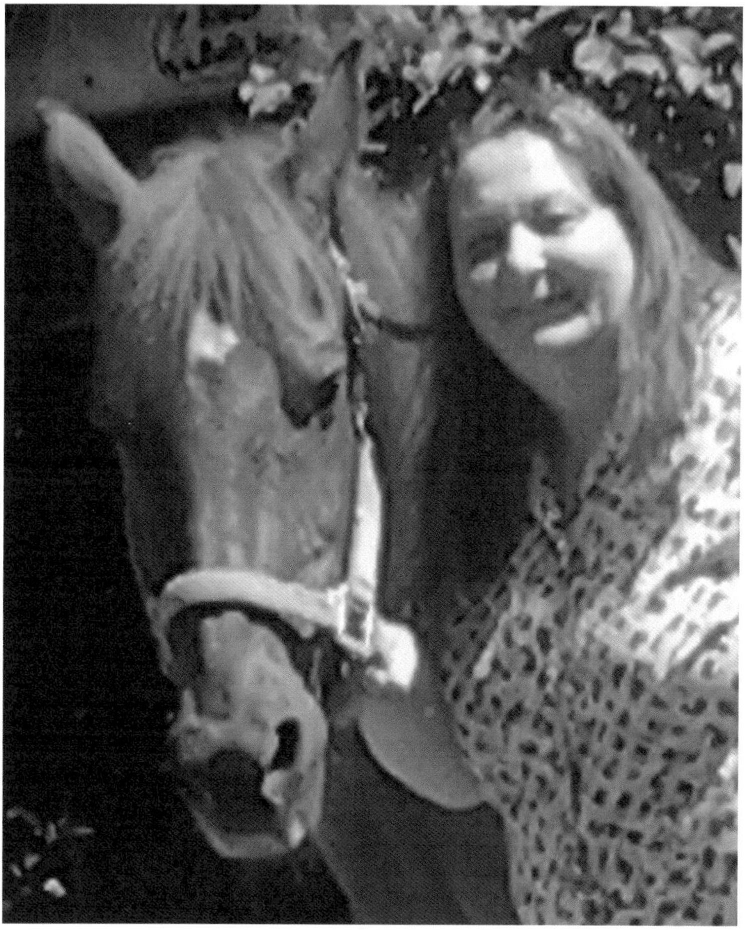

Denise Shumaker

Hi! I am Denise Shumaker. I grew up near Moonshine, Illinois, on a sustainable farm in the house where my father was born. I have always loved animals and had a deep interest in farm life. Over the years I have been known to take in many strays, and according to my mom, my husband was one of them.

I have a BS in education from Eastern Illinois University with a major in art and natural sciences. I have had an interest in writing since grade school. When I was in third grade, one of my poems and artworks was chosen and published in the statewide school news magazine. Since then I have only written pieces for myself, for my grandchildren, and classes that I have taught or taken. I have written poetry, an alternate book about a snake for my grandchildren, and a children's story about the differences between a frog and a toad for a science class.

The two 55-word stories titled "The Love of my Life" and "Sophie" are true stories about the most beloved animals I saved. I rescued Buster before he was taken to the pound. Sophie was slated to be sold to the killers. Both of these animals changed our family's lives for the better. Buster delighted our family with his playful antics, and Sophie helped many people with disabilities for sixteen years. I could tell you more about their lives but that is another story....

Mayhem

Kimberly Sweeney

Okay, let's talk about body parts. But first of all I want to say that if I get to be reincarnated, I am coming back as a capital M, capital A, capital N — that spells MAN! Not WO-MAN. MAN!

Just tell me what's so great about the bodies of women. We were made from the rib of a man if you believe in a supreme being, the Almighty God. In addition, we must pay the price of original sin. Thank you, Evie. You just had to taste the fruit from that tree, didn't you? You just could not leave it alone. Maybe eventually Adam would have tasted it! Instead, women are now cursed from the very beginning.

But I am getting off point. If you are born a female, the first ten to twelve years of your life is ignorant bliss and physical freedom. Then the mayhem starts: the cramps, the bloating, the headaches, the migraines, the raging hormones, the psychotic episodes, the chocoholic frenzies, the food binges, the tiredness. Thirty days later, it starts again! Some of us take birth control pills to regulate all this monthly mayhem and to keep from getting pregnant. The birth control pills only regulate when the mayhem will come each month. They do not control all the physical symptoms. Some women have their mayhem for a whole week although there are those fortunate enough to only have it three days. Or so I've heard. For some reason unbeknownst to man, redheads have a tendency to bleed more. I'm a redhead.

When I was growing up, my household consisted of my mother, my two sisters, and me—four women—in addition to my father and two brothers. Four against three. Plus, it is said that women who live together all get their mayhem around the same time. Yup, that was true in my household. God Bless my father and brothers—during this time of month none of them could do anything right. They might as well have lived on another planet because it was war, baby. Men were the enemies and they could never understand what we females were going through each month. We didn't even know why we were angry at the world. No wonder my older brother stayed in his room with the door shut all the time. However, my father always said he should have bought stock in the female monthly supply industry because he would have been a millionaire by now.

After the mayhem and the babies (if you have children), we as women look forward to the time when the mayhem will go away for good. We talk about that day even in our teens. Good riddance. Happy trails to you. And then, just when life is supposed to be great and the mayhem over—surprise! Here come the raging hormones, the night sweats, the power surges, the insomnia, the fatigue, and the small fans sitting on your office desk all seasons of the year for the next TEN years! Yes, I said the next TEN years. Hooray for menopause! This is God's funny little joke on Evie for eating the forbidden fruit. So the next time you are lying in bed in the middle of the night drenched in sweat and your hair is all wet from those freaking hot flashes, you can scream at Evie and thank her for the physical mayhem we women have had to put up with our whole lives. Please, don't even get me started on bladder infections.

Best Friends

Kimberly Sweeney

Nose to paw, eyes to soul, you stole my heart. Tails wagging, feet tapping, you greeted me at the door each day. For fifteen years you protected us all and loved us unconditionally. Fur to hand so soft and comforting—love soaked up. Rest in Peace Sasha and Smokey, until we meet on Rainbow Bridge.

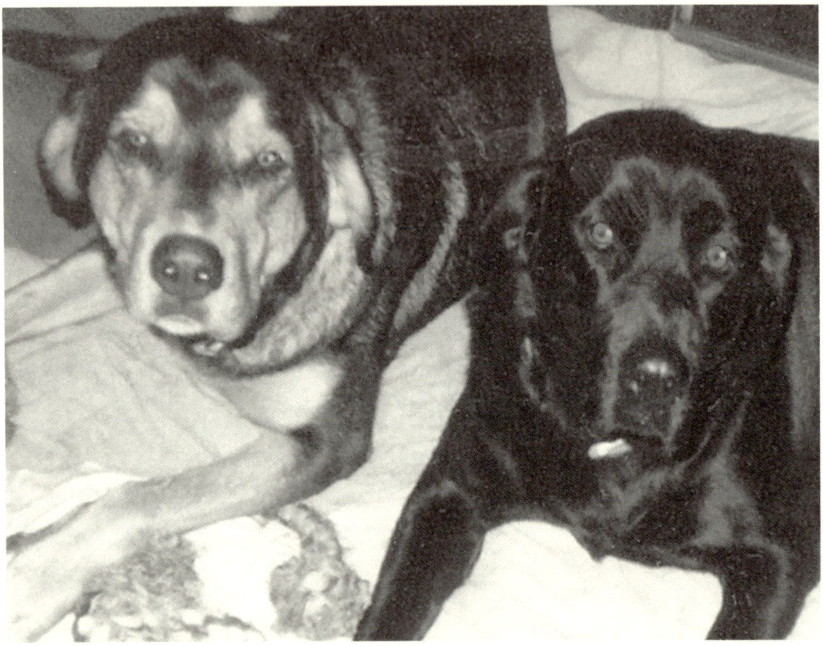

Kimberly Sweeney

I was born and raised in Charleston, Illinois. I met the love of my life while in college and we reside in Charleston where we have been married for thirty-six adventurous years and have three grown artistic and beautiful children. They encourage and motivate me to keep writing.

I am fourth in the line of five children. My father was an avid writer and musician. He instilled in me my love for writing and music. Whenever any of us kids missed school and needed a note to get back in, he didn't just write so-and-so was sick with the flu. He wrote a two- or three-page dissertation on why we were not in school. The school administrators and principals loved his writings. They were humorous, informative, and totally humiliating to the child he wrote about. I now wish he had left a copy of all those letters so we could still read them today and pass them along for future family generations.

I received my bachelor's degree in English and a minor in music from Eastern Illinois University, and I've been writing poetry since the fifth grade. In 2008, I took an adult course in memoir writing with Dr. Daiva Markelis, professor of creative writing at EIU. Thus began my journey into memoir writing. It has been an awe-inspiring journey with all these writers, and my family now learns about my childhood, heritage, and life.

I would like to leave you with my favorite quote by Maya Angelou, which sums up memoir writing for me so eloquently:

I would have my ears filled
with the world's music...
Let me hear all sounds of life and living.

Relections of an Immigrant:
First Years

Luz M. Whittenbarger

"We are flying now over Colombian territory," said the pilot. Mi patria, I thought. My country. It was my return journey after six months of study in Washington, DC, completing my architecture degree. After living in a foreign land, love of home becomes very real. My roots were thirsty for the nourishment of the fruits of Colombia, of family, lifelong friends, and traditions. As I gazed at the tail end of the sunset from the window, I saw magic — the northern border of Colombia was defined by millions of lights from city ports on the Atlantic! Through the descending shadows, the majestic beauty of the Andes mountains showed their ragged surfaces, dotted with lights of little villages, the meandering roads and the rivers that converge into the long artery, the Magdalena River that runs south to north, as do most rivers in the southern hemisphere.

Ev, a professor at Michigan State University, sat next to me on the plane. He told me his wife wanted to learn to play the tiple, a small guitar-like instrument native to Colombia. I offered to teach her and we became good friends. At their home one evening, something happened that affected the rest of my life: I saw Bob again after having met him briefly the previous year.

Destiny at Play

In August of the same year, Bob and I married. He was from Indiana. He had come to Bogotá, the capital of Colombia, to teach English for the United States Binational Center in 1960. While at a bank one day, he saw a confused gringo named Gene H. Bob offered his assistance, and after learning that Gene's wife and newborn baby would soon arrive in Bogotá, and that the contract to his apartment had been sold to a higher bidder, Bob offered his.

Baby Julie's crib was wheeled out of the second bedroom to the living room nightly so Bob could sleep. Soon they found a large house and became a happy family that included my future husband, "Lilo" to little Julie. Gene was a professor at the University of Wisconsin doing research for the Land Tenure Center in Bogotá. He offered Bob a research assistantship and became his graduate advisor. Gene was also Bob's best man at our wedding.

Bob's parents flew to Bogotá to be at our wedding. They talked about the wonderful things they saw and experienced and also of my family. Being such sensitive and polite people, they constantly did everything possible to make me feel loved and at home. I could always count on them and on our friends to surround us with their positive feelings about Colombia.

Bob was interested in every aspect of Colombian life. He made many friends, both gringos and Colombians, wealthy and poor; he thought the weather was perfect in Bogotá at 8,600 feet above sea level and four degrees north of the equator. The topography, diverse climate, and warmth of its people made him love Colombia. The fact that many señoritas of marrying age gave him their attentions made his stay even more alluring.

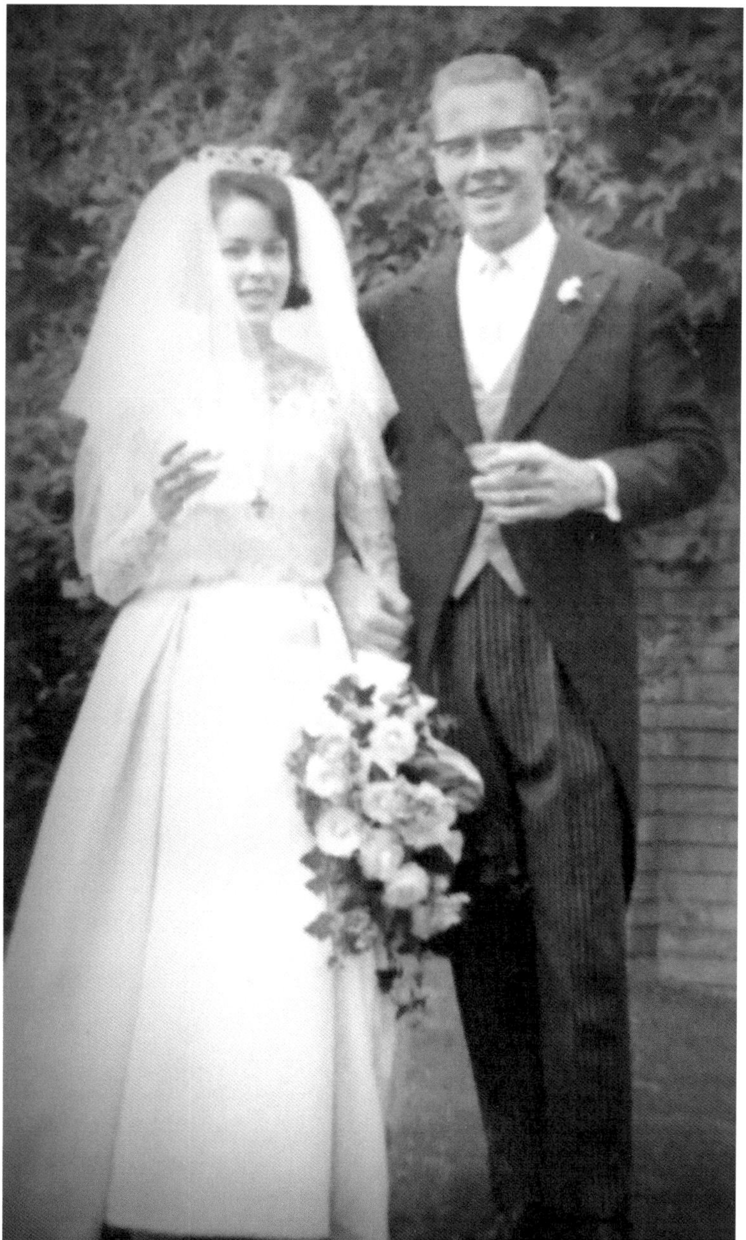

Who is a "Gringo" in Colombia: A Cultural Note

It is important to explain the term gringo, for I believe most North Americans understand it as derogatory. In Colombia, however, it is simply used to describe someone born in another country. It can even be used as an endearing term—I call Bob "my gringo" or "my gringuito" (little gringo) at times.

Returning to the United States as a Bride: First Culture Shock

My brother, who walked me down the aisle, said good-bye with tears in his eyes as we boarded the plane to Miami the next day. Father had passed away two years before. It was in Miami when I was first addressed as Mrs. Robert Whittenbarger. Where was I? My first and last names disappeared! At that time I resented this. I felt this system of address dismissed the woman in the equation. In Colombia a married woman keeps her maiden name, in my case Soler; she then adds her husband's last name. Thus my new married name would have been Luz Maria Soler de Whittenbarger, "de" meaning married to.

My father was a lawyer. We enjoyed upper middle-class status: private schools, maids, a summer home, cars, etc. In Latin America, social class is not measured only by the economic indicators; purity of lineage is as important. Perhaps that is the reason preserving last names after marriage is so important.

A Way of Life Back Then

Life was carefree in Bogotá. I used to go to my office each day and after work enjoyed tea with friends, a concert or ballet performance, a swim or tennis match at the club. Sometimes I simply went home, hopped in my parents' bed with my mother and whichever of my siblings was around, and chatted about our day. The maid would serve us "cafesito" (demitasse coffee). We watched TV and waited for our father to head to the dining room to be served dinner around eight p.m.

Oh, How I Miss You

I missed my mother's advice and love. Chatting often with lifelong friends was no longer possible. Familiar aromas, food, and flavors were now far removed; singing along with the radio songs I learned by heart was not possible. Besides, when I played Colombian music, the joy came accompanied with nostalgia and a few burning tears. (It still does). I danced to my music with my shadow again and again, although when Bob was around, we danced together. Knowing Colombia is a big part of Bob's history is of great comfort to me.

Now I Live in the United States of America

I learned to be a good homemaker and citizen although I was still greatly influenced by my upbringing. We bought rubber gloves and cleaning supplies — Bob read and translated the instructions for me and also learned a few new things himself. *Cooking for Two* by Betty Crocker became my bible. It taught me ways to prepare food and how many ingredients to use; I learned that one pound of spaghetti was too much for just two people. Using leftovers became a science. I never dreamed I would eat the same food twice the same week. Disguising leftovers became my challenge. Actually, I love to cook now.

Carrying the dirty clothesbasket to the laundry room in our student-housing basement was a particularly embarrassing chore for me. I had never done the laundry! I was still conditioned to believe this was the maid's job. Besides, I did not completely understand the washer or detergent instructions — Bob sometimes had to wear pink underwear or bleached dark socks.

Answering the phone always required a moment of prayer while I asked for divine intervention. It had been six weeks since our wedding, and understanding English was my biggest challenge. Even though Bob is completely proficient in Spanish, he only spoke English to me. My favorite TV program was *I Love Lucy*. It helped me understand colloquial vocabulary and marital situations. And Ricky Ricardo had my kind of accent!

Work and Leisure: New Ways

Our income was mainly the GI Bill check, Bob's assistantship, and soon, my work doing engineering drafting. My training in architecture and interior design was paying off. It was great being in contact with co-workers and trying out my English skills in addition to bringing home about three times the income of my husband. Our budget occasionally permitted us to have pizza and a pitcher of draft beer or "all-you-can-eat fish" for $1.99. We loved these "gourmet" outings because we went with friends and they had a ball. I say "they" because to me it seemed everyone spoke in tongues. I elbowed Bob constantly for I could not understand their jokes, slang, or puns. When Bob said something, everyone laughed. He is well known for his puns. Sometimes he would translate for me, but translated jokes make no sense most of the time.

Student Housing

The campus of the University of Wisconsin at Madison is beautiful. Lake Mendota is constantly host to motor- and sailboats, skaters, and fishermen; it is bordered with nature preserves and beautiful beaches. It reflects the hilly terrain and beautiful, old, ivy-covered buildings. The way to our married-student-housing area was a long sloping avenue lined by old maples — their foliage hid the sky in the summer and their fall colors provided a glorious journey home from campus. There, we enjoyed a new one-bedroom apartment and a brand-new colicky baby next door, a community center that was really a cosmopolitan center offering programs for families, a cooperative babysitting exchange, and a food cooperative in which husbands and wives volunteered their work to maintain low prices on grocery items direct from farmers. The concept of potluck suppers was new to me, and I enjoyed the many flavors and sometimes exotic dishes international students prepared. I learned about casseroles and pies. Do you know that the word "pie" in Spanish means foot?

Profanities

My first boss was the engineer and land surveyor "Spike" Carlson, a former mayor of Madison and a war veteran who had not forgotten the language used in the barracks. When talking with his field men, he used some words familiar to me. He would say "God" and "Jesus Christ" with such strength and frequency that I admired him for his faith. At home I repeated these words to Bob who, appalled, patiently explained that this was unacceptable in this culture, especially coming from women.

"Fertility Acres"

It had been one and a half years since our wedding and I no longer worked full time because our first baby was on its way. I now took art classes and learned about motherhood. I socialized a lot and read about becoming a good mother. Although I did not have the luxury of the help of a nurse to care for the baby at night, becoming a mother was life at its best!

The university contributes some of its unused land for married students to plant their individual twenty-five-square-foot gardens each spring. Bob and I decided to plant our own: lettuce, carrots, tomatoes, radishes, melons, beans, and peas.

That year Bob registered at Indiana University in Bloomington for summer courses. My Colombian friend Virginia came to be with me. The care of the garden was my responsibility. As my waist was growing, so were the weeds in the garden. Virginia and I managed; actually, I thoroughly enjoyed this bucolic experience. Me using a hoe? Pulling weeds? Getting dirt under my fingernails? Rolling and unrolling the water hose? The warm sun, the sense of community, the hope and renewal of Mother Earth in its process from seeds to fruit let me experience nature as I had never before. God was at work in many fronts. Life is a miracle!

Bob phoned me every night. He wanted a detailed report about the progress of our baby. When I first heard his heartbeat and was aware of his movements and told Bob about them, he was impatient to return and share life in progress.

Fall came again—my second. Trees are not deciduous in the tropics. What a spectacle of color! In a way, fall saddens me. Such magnificence is the announcement of winter. The sound of crushed dry leaves under my feet always seemed like a good-bye scream. But we were elated welcoming our first child. Would our baby be able to survive winter? He was born late November; there was snow on the ground. Inexperience caused us to wrap our precious bundle in excess out of the hospital. He was perspiring when we arrived home.

North American Women and Celebrations I Love

Dios mio! "They" are so incredible! "They" keep house, are good wives, mothers, daughters-in-law, friends, sisters, cooks, lovers to their husbands. Many work outside the home and attend meetings, do volunteer work, and go to church. They graciously entertain and their fingernails look nice! Oh, I get tired just thinking about it.

Trying to become active in the community, I joined a group of International Wives. There were presentations about American traditions. It was Christmastime; a cookie exchange had been planned. I chose to bake lemon cookies. I baked for hours. When I arrived with my large box and saw all others holding only a small plate, I realized I had mistaken two dozen for twelve dozen!

In Latin America, Easter is a strictly religious celebration. I love the Easter Bunny and Halloween, and how little children enjoy their costumes and traditions with their families. Thanksgiving and the Fourth of July are also beautiful traditions.

Another Cultural Shock: Punctuality

We were invited somewhere at six p.m. I relaxed and did other things than being ready. Ten minutes before the hour, I chose my clothes and slowly started making myself up. One hour later, Bob, beside himself, told me: "This has to change. It is not polite to arrive late." You see, in Colombia it is understood that guests arrive one hour or so after the stated time for a social engagement. It has taken a real effort on my part to learn to be on time in the USA, where every minute counts. Often I feel enslaved by the clock.

These are only a few memories of the early years out of the fifty I have lived in this country. There are so many more. Many hundreds of people have contributed to what I am today. My heart is larger for there has always been room to love another experience, another person, and another possibility. I am so lucky to have been welcomed as a citizen of two beautiful countries, to understand their languages, and to embrace life in both. Life is indeed wonderful.

Luz M. Whittenbarger

As an immigrant, I've had a treasure trove of experiences that have enriched my life in untold ways. I was born in Bogotá, Colombia. I was educated in a Catholic school, studied interior design, and later did coursework in architecture at Universidad America. In the fall of 1963 I came to the USA and was accepted at Syracuse University to finish architecture. I missed my family and in January of 1964 I returned home. There I met and married Bob fifty wonderful years ago.

There was no guesswork as to how I should behave growing up; rules were followed, social and family traditions were clear, and the love of friends and family made my world carefree.

While a wife and the mother of two wonderful sons, I continued my interest in the arts, always taking one more class. Worldwide traveling has been one of my passions, as is documenting life with my digital camera. I received a Jefferson Award for Public Service in 2005.

After receiving my BA at Eastern Illinois University in 1980, I taught Spanish part time at Lakeland College before beginning my full-time career at Charleston High School. After that I joined the Foreign Languages Department at EIU as a part-time instructor.

It is real; my story is part of this book! Involvement with the Past~Forward memoir group has given me wings. Thank you all for your encouragement and support! And perhaps I should thank the shadow of my mother, who was a prolific published poet and strengthened my love of writing.

The Customer

Jacqui Worden

At noon she said, "My mother has to give up all her china. I asked, 'What would you like, Mom?'"
"Some beautiful bowls."

The customer gathered and nested them: tan, brown, green, yellow, celadon, blue. "Two are for me!"

Midafternoon she returned. "Need two more! I asked Mom to choose. She said, 'I want them ALL.'"

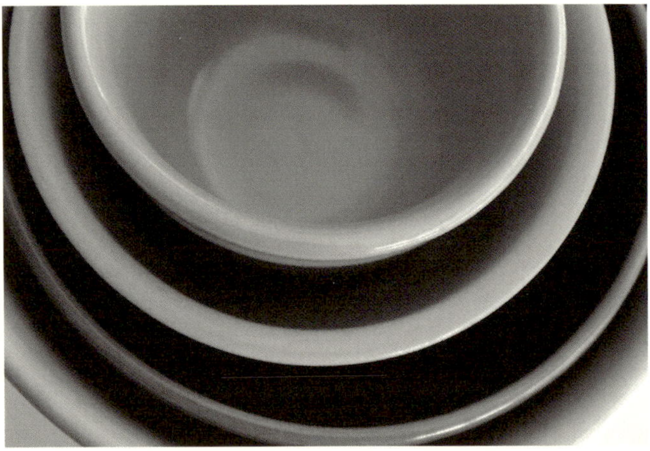

New Home

Jacqui Worden

First, a small one. Next bowl's blue, then brown. Another holds a carved flower. Fifth one's for cereal; finally, a classic celadon.

With the bowls nesting one inside the other, the woman smiled. Her mother might have to give up her china in her new assisted-living home, but she wouldn't be without Beauty.

Jacqui Worden

I'VE BEEN A naturalist, a newspaper columnist, a reference librarian, an art teacher, a U.S. Census enumerator, and an entrepreneur. As a child I made and sold potholders, going door-to-door, even taking orders to complement my neighbors' kitchens. Now, as a ceramicist, I often sell my creations, including colorful one-of-a-kind bowls, at art fairs. You can read more about my work at www.craftleagueofcu.org/worden.

Photo Credits

Daiva Markelis
Photograph courtesy of the author.

Above the Beach
Photograph of courtesy of the author.

Presbyterian Surprise
Photograph from First Presbyterian archives.

A Nostalgic Passion
Photographs courtesy of the author and Save the Will Rogers Theater.

The Menu
Photograph courtesy of the author.

Phyllis Bayles
Photograph by Duke Bagger.

A Very Dark Day in Charleston, Illinois, History
Illustration from *'Round the Square*, permission of Nancy Easter Shick.

Bob Clapp
Photograph courtesy of the author.

Wonderland Under
Photograph by Gaye Harrison.

Testament
Photograph by Gaye Harrison.

Lois Dickenson
Photograph by Gaye Harrison.

A New World
Collage by Mary Dwiggins.

Keeping Time
Collage by Gaye Harrison.

Mary Dwiggins
Photograph courtesy of the author.

The Civil War and My Ancestors
Photograph courtesy of the author.

My Mother
Photographs courtesy of the author.

Hannah Eads
Photograph by Gaye Harrison.

La Grange Park
Photographs courtesy of the author.

Dad
Photograph courtesy of the author.

Marty Gabriel
Photograph courtesy of the author.

Harryetta
Photograph courtesy of the author.

Renaissance
Photograph courtesy of the author.

Jane Cavins Gilbert
Photograph by Gaye Harrison.

San Francisco Penny
Photograph and drawing by Gaye Harrison.

Gaye Harrison
Photograph courtesy of the author.

The Most Amazing Lady I Have Ever Known
Photograph courtesy of the author.

Dorothy Helland
Photograph courtesy of the author.

Paddling to Canada
Drawing by Gaye Harrison.

Bill Heyduck
Photograph by Gaye Harrison.

Windows
Photograph by Gaye Harrison.

Madeline Ignazito
Photograph by Gaye Harrison.

More Blessed to Give Than to Receive
Photograph courtesy of the author.

Love and Marriage
Photograph by Gaye Harrison.

Helen Krehbiel-Reed
Photograph by Gaye Harrison.

Happy Trails
Photograph courtesy of the author.

Photographs
Photograph courtesy of the author.

Amy Lynch
Photograph courtesy of the author.

A Hair-Raising Experience
Drawing by Gaye Harrison.

Old Blue Eyes
Photograph courtesy of the author.

Janet Messenger
Photograph courtesy of the author.

Bob and Tom
Drawing by Gaye Harrison.

My Special Shoes
Photograph of shoes by Gaye Harrison.

Johnni Olds
Photograph by Gaye Harrison.

Afghan
Photograph by Gaye Harrison.

Peggy Perkins
Photograph by Gaye Harrison.

Eddie Thompson
Photograph from iStockPhoto.com.

David R. Pollard
Photograph courtesy of the author.

How I Learned to Play Guitar Off the TV
Photograph courtesy of the author.

Turquoise and Race Horses
Photograph courtesy of the author.

Julie Rea
Photograph by Gaye Harrison.

Sophie
Photograph courtesy of the author.

Denise Shumaker
Photograph by Gaye Harrison.

Best Friends
Photograph courtesy of the author.

Kimberly Sweeney
Photograph by Gaye Harrison.

Reflections of an Immigrant: First Years
Photograph courtesy of the author.

Luz M. Whittenbarger
Photograph courtesy of the author.

New Home
Photograph from iStockPhoto.com.

Jacqui Worden
Photograph by Gaye Harrison.

Interested in joining Past~Forward?

There are no prerequisites for joining, only an interest in writing memoirs. For more information please feel free to contact Janet Messenger at jmess1@consolidated.net or Daiva Markelis at dmmarkelis@eiu.edu.